May Riley Smith

Sometime

And Other Poems

May Riley Smith

Sometime
And Other Poems

ISBN/EAN: 9783744709538

Printed in Europe, USA, Canada, Australia, Japan

Cover: Foto ©Thomas Meinert / pixelio.de

More available books at **www.hansebooks.com**

SOMETIME

AND OTHER POEMS

BY

MAY RILEY SMITH

NEW YORK

E. P. DUTTON AND COMPANY

31 WEST TWENTY-THIRD STREET

1897

Press of J. J. Little & Co.
Astor Place, New York

To him whose praises make my heart more vain
    Than any recompense my life can know,
Whose patient hands, through every doubt and pain,
    Make easy places where my feet may go; .
And to the child, whose life has been to me
    The sweetest flower my bosom ever wore,
Whose little elbow leans upon my knee, —
    The lightest burden mother ever bore! —
To these, the sharers of my household throne,
    Whose names within my prayers together stand,
I dedicate what always is their own, —
    The pleasant labor of my unskilled hand.

CONTENTS.

8 *Contents.*

Contents.

SOMETIME.

OMETIME, when all life's les-
sons have been learned,
And sun and stars forever-
more have set,
The things which our weak judgments
here have spurned,
The things o'er which we grieved with
lashes wet,
Will flash before us out of life's dark
night,
As stars shine most in deeper tints of
blue;
And we shall see how all God's plans
are right,
And how what seemed reproof was
love most true.

And we shall see how, while we frown
    and sigh,
  God's plans go on as best for you
    and me, —
How, when we called, he needed not
    our cry,
  Because his wisdom to the end could
    see.
And even as wise parents disallow
  Too much of sweet to craving baby-
    hood, —
So God, perhaps, is keeping from us
    now
  Life's sweetest things, because it seem-
    eth good.

And if sometimes, commingled with
    life's wine,
  We find the wormwood, and rebel and
    shrink,
Be sure a wiser hand than yours or mine
  Pours out this potion for our lips to
    drink.

And if some friend you love is lying
   low,
  Where human kisses cannot reach his
    face,
Oh, do not blame the loving Father so,
  But wear your sorrow with obedient
    grace!

And you shall shortly know that length-
   ened breath
  Is not the sweetest gift God sends his
    friend;
And that sometimes the sable pall of
   death
  Conceals the fairest boon his love
    can send.
If we could push ajar the gates of life,
  And stand within and all God's work-
    ings see,
We could interpret all this doubt and
   strife,
  And for each mystery could find a
    key!

But not to-day. Then be content, poor
    heart !
  God's plans, like lilies pure and white,
    unfold ;
We must not tear the close-shut leaves
    apart, —
  Time will reveal the chalices of gold.
And if, through patient toil, we reach
    the land
  Where tired feet, with sandals loosed,
    may rest,
When we shall clearly see and under-
    stand,
  I think that we will say, " God knew
    the best ! "

"YE HAVE DONE IT UNTO ME."

TREMBLING she stood at the
heavenly door, —
The world around her was
strange and new;
She had come through the dark from
the earthly shore,
And how should a pilgrim know what
to do, —
Whether to knock, or whether to wait,
When she finds herself at the shining
Gate?

"Thou hast crossed the Valley," an
angel said,
Touching the pilgrim's dampened
hair, —

"The lonely valley which travellers
  dread,
  As hither they wend from the land
    of Care.
Wouldst thou greet the King? Dost
    wear his sign?
Hast thou steadfast held to thy faith
    and shrine?"

"It is many a year," the pilgrim sighed,
  "Since I have thought upon faith
    and creed;
The burdened and poor at my threshold
    cried ;
  Had I time to study my lesser need?
And when I would pray for my own
    soul's good,
They interrupted with cries for food.

"I should lift my head from the Father's
    breast,
  If I were in heaven, and heard their
    cry ;

How could I selfishly take my rest,
  Thinking of wearier ones than I?
I would slip from the ranks of the
    undefiled
To comfort the woes of a little child!"

"Peace! Has the Father forsaken his
    throne?"
  The angel answered with stern sur-
    prise.
"Has his arm grown short, that he
    needs thy own, —
  Have the woes of the world escaped
    his eyes?
But see! the Master himself draws
    near, —
Thy foolish story hath reached his ear."

The woman lifted her troubled brow,
  And the mists of earth from her
    spirit fell;
No stranger's face did she gaze on
    now, —

She knew the Christ; she had loved
    Him well;
She had met those eyes, with their
    tender grace,
On the earth in many a suffering face!

They had often looked from a beggar's
    hood,
    From under a motherless baby's hair;
They had pierced her often, reproached
    her, wooed, —
    Had beckoned her here, had followed
    her there;
In many and many a strange disguise
· She had met the gaze of those pleading
    eyes!

His voice was sweet to the tired one;
    His touch was balm to her down-bent
    head, —
"What thou to the least of my poor
    hast done,

Thou hast done unto me," he gently
said.
"In my Father's house there are many
rooms;"
And He led her in from the earthly
glooms.

WHEN WE PRAY.

AS tired children go at candle-
    light, —
  The glow in their young eyes
    quenched with the sun,
Almost too languid, now that play is
    done,
To seek their father's knee, and say
    " good-night," —
So, to our greater Father out of sight,
  When the brief gamut of the day is
    run,
  Defeats endured, and petty triumphs
    won,
We kneel and listlessly his care invite.

Then, with no sense of gain, — no tender thrill,
As when we leave the presence of a
  friend;
No lingering content our souls to
  steep, —
But reckoning our gains and losses still,
We turn the leaf upon the dull day's
  end,
And, oarless, drift out to the sea of
  sleep.

CROSS-PURPOSES.

WHAT sorrow we should beckon
    unawares,
  What stinging nettles in our
    path would grow,
If God should answer all our thought-
    less prayers,
  Or bring to harvest the poor seed we
    sow!

The storm for which you prayed, whose
    kindly shock
  Revived your fields and blessed the
    fainting air,
Drove a strong ship upon the cruel
    rock,
  And one I loved went down in ship-
    wreck there.

I ask for sunshine on my grapes to-day;
  You plead for rain to kiss your
    drooping flowers;
And thus within God's patient hand we
    lay
  These intricate cross-purposes of ours.

I greeted with cold grace and doubting
    fears
The guest who proved an angel at my
    side;
And I have shed more bitter, burning
    tears
Because of hopes fulfilled than prayers
    denied.

Then be not clamorous, O restless soul,
  But hold thy trust in God's eternal
    plan;
He views our life's dull weaving as a
    whole, —
  Only its tangled threads are seen by
    man!

Dear Lord, vain repetitions are not meet
    When we would bring our messages
        to thee;
Help us to lay them, then, at thy dear
        feet
In acquiescence, not garrulity.

MY UNINVITED GUEST.

ONE day there entered at my
chamber door
A presence whose light foot-
fall on the floor
No token gave; and, ere I could with-
stand,
Within her clasp she drew my trembling
hand.

"Intrusive guest," I cried, "my palm I
lend
But to the gracious pressure of a
friend!
Why comest thou, unbidden and in
gloom,
Trailing thy cold gray garments in my
room?

"I know thee, Pain! Thou art the sul-
    len foe
Of every sweet enjoyment here below;
Thou art the comrade and ally of Death,
And timid mortals shrink from thy cold
    breath.

"No fragrant balms grow in thy garden
    beds,
Nor slumbrous poppies droop their
    crimson heads;
And well I know thou comest to me
    now
To bind thy burning chains upon my
    brow!"

And though my puny will stood
    straightly up,
From that day forth I drank her pun-
    gent cup,
And ate her bitter bread, — with leaves
    of rue,
Which in her sunless gardens rankly
    grew.

And now, so long it is, I scarce can
tell
When Pain within my chamber came to
dwell;
And though she is not fair of mien or
face,
She hath attracted to my humble place

A company most gracious and refined,
Whose touches are like balm, whose
voices kind:
Sweet Sympathy, with box of ointment
rare;
Courage, who sings while she sits
weaving there;

Brave Patience, whom my heart esteem-
eth much,
And who hath wondrous virtue in her
touch.
Such is the chaste and sweet society
Which Pain, my faithful foe, hath
brought to me.

And now upon my threshold there she
    stands,
Reaching to me her rough yet kindly
    hands
In silent truce.   Thus for a time we
    part,
And a great gladness overflows my
    heart;

For she is so ungentle in her way
That no host welcomes her or bids her
    stay;
Yet, though men bolt and bar their
    house from thee,
To every door, O Pain, thou hast a key!

HIS NAME.

WHEN I shall go where my
Redeemer is,
In the far City, on the other
side,
And at the threshold of his palaces
Shall loose my sandals, ever to abide,
I know my Heavenly King will smiling
wait
To give me welcome as I reach the
gate.

Oh, joy! oh, bliss! for I shall see his
face,
And wear his blessed Name upon my
brow, —
That Name which stands for pardon,
love, and grace, —

That Name before which every knee
    shall bow;
No music half so sweet can ever be,
As that dear Name which he shall
    write for me!

Crowned with this royal signet, I shall
    walk
  With lifted forehead through the
      eternal street,
And with a holier mien and gentler
    talk
  Will tell my story to the friends I
      meet, —
Of how the King did stoop his Name
    to write
Upon my brow in characters of light.

Then, till I go to meet my Father's
    smile,
  I 'll keep my forehead smooth from
      passion's scars, —

From angry frowns that trample and
defile,
And every sin that desecrates and
mars,
That I may lift a face unflushed with
shame,
Whereon my Lord may write his holy
Name!

IF THIS WERE TWENTY CENTURIES AGO.

F this were twenty centuries
    ago,
And three wise men should
    seek my house, and say:
"We bring glad tidings! Christ is
    born to-day;
Arise, and follow yonder star, whose
    glow
Will lead you to the child!"— would I
    obey,
If this were twenty centuries ago?

From out my urn of precious, hoarded
    things
Would I make haste to pour the richest
    share

For him? The sweetest of my per-
    fumes spare
To bathe the feet of the young King of
    kings?
Or break the costliest ointment on his
    hair
From out my urn of precious, hoarded
    things?

Alas! I dare not say this would I do,
Since I have slighted many another
    guest
That came from God, — have stayed
    from many a quest
That would have led me to the good
    and true,
To slumber on with head upon my
    breast;
Nay, nay! I dare not say this would I do.

My best resolves like shifting shadows
    are;
Each day some holy light shines on
    unsought, —

And while my silly, fluttering wings are
    caught
By the world's rosy candle, Christ's
    own star —
How can I tell? — might beckon me for
    naught;
My best resolves like shifting shadows
    are.

And when Christ comes again, — as
    come he will —
And wise ones hasten forth with rapt
    delight
To welcome him, and own his kingly
    right,
Will men be questioning and doubting
    still,
As when upon that first, far Christmas
    night, —
When Christ shall come again, — as
    come he will?

THE SLIGHTED FLOWERS.

HE slept; and the dream of
    Heaven
    With its rapturous surprise,
Had folded the silken lashes
    Over the tender eyes;
And the peace which passeth knowl-
    edge
    Seemed, to our mortal sight,
To circle the pallid forehead
    With a ring of holy light.

She lay while we piled the lilies,
    Like drifts of odorous snow,
On the breast whose thoughts were
    whiter
    Than milkiest flowers that blow.

We braided them in her tresses,
　Their petals caressed her face,
But she who had loved the lilies
　Was heedless now of their grace.

She slighted the timid beauty
　Of violets, chaste and sweet,
That trailed like a purple ribbon
　From girdle to unshod feet.
And she uttered no word of chiding,
　When we crushed a rose in our hand;
So we knew by these silent tokens
　She had gone to the Unknown Land.

MARY WAKEFIELD.

GAINST the painted hell of Angelo
I set this living picture of despair:
A burning ship, strong men distraught with woe,
Rough seamen's oaths, which meant not oaths, but prayer;
White pleading faces, little children's cries,
And women's arms flung upward to the skies!

Along the burning deck a woman
    sped
  While the red horror close and closer
    pressed
Until its hot breath scorched her baby's
    head,
  Hiding itself within her throbbing
    breast;
When, shrinking backward from the
    flames' mad kiss,
She reeled into the water's black abyss!

Poor mother! Was it granted her to
    see,
  Ere sight was veiled by the engulfing
    wave,
The noble girl whose arms so lustily
  Wrested from her the babe she could
    not save;
And dared, in a baptismal scene so
    wild,
To stand as sponsor to this orphaned
    child?

And this was Mary Wakefield. Daunt-
less girl,
Who, with a child across her shoulder
thrown,
Set out to wage with death against the
whirl
Of those mad waves, hand-fettered
and alone !
A deed that gave her right to stand erect
With seraphim, nor show them disre-
spect !

With one firm hand she held against
the tide
The sobbing child. The other tightly
grasped
A fender swinging from the steamer's
side,
By a stout cable to the railing clasped ;
She drew the heavy beam on inch by
inch
Toward the nearest flame, nor did she
flinch

Though the hot tongues came hissing
    at her brow.
  With patient toil she guided on the
    rope
To where the flame could bite at it; and
    now
  She has the joyful answer to her hope!
It burns asunder, and the heavy beam
Drops down before her into the black
    stream!

Upon this strange steed's back she then
    set down
  The little child. And pushing on
    before
Holding between her teeth the baby's
    gown,
  She struck out bravely for the distant
    shore,
A league away, with well-aimed, steady
    strides,
While on its dripping steed the baby
    rides!

As rose and fell the girl's white oars,
      the rain
   Thrummed its dull monotone. The
      thunders rolled
Their heavy drums.   The wind swept
      a refrain.
   Some distant bells the hour of mid-
      night told.
And now and then the lightning's vivid
      thread
Through the thick darkness wove a
      seam of red !

Strong men went shuddering down to
      death that night,
   Whose arms were like to knitted
      strands of steel,
While this slight girl waged an unequal
      fight
   For two — making no loud appeal
To God, but praying mutely with her
      arms,
Seeking the while to sooth the child's
      alarms !

"Hush, little one!   Home is not far
    away,
  And I am here holding you by your
    gown,   ·
Just as old Rover holds you when at
    play;
  And with my strong arms plashing
    up and down,
I make your queer horse gallop to the
    shore,
And baby shall be cold and wet no
    more!"

Then, with a tenderness almost divine,
  She tried to thrust a merry nursery
    song
Through her shut teeth; and while
    each panting line.
  Smote on her jaded breath like smart-
    ing thong,
I think God ringed her with an unseen
    crown,
And every face in heaven bent softly
    down!

And thus she won the shore. There on
    the sands
A seaman lay, half naked, cold and
    faint.
Unfastening her gown with shivering
    hands,
She laid it on him. Then this gentle
    saint
Lifted the sleeping baby to her breast,
And toiled, half-fainting, to a place of
    rest!

THE WEARY MODEL.

NE day, an artist in his studio,
  Upon his model draped a
    quaint old gown,
Of some rare Indian stuff, wove long
    ago
  Of countless mellow shades of gold
    and brown, —
Sunshine and shadow, like the shining
    hair
That Raphael made his sweet Madonnas
    wear.

Silent and passive, as if carved of stone,
  Stood the young model in her love-
    liness;

For now the tireless artist sought alone
  To paint the gold-brown shimmer of
    the dress;
Nor must she stir the robe which flashed
    and shone, —
Hers to be patient and be wrought
    upon.

At last the sinuous folds were all com-
    plete;
  Like a soft wave they bathed the
    pliant girl,
And, rippling from the shoulders to the
    feet,
  Fell on the carpet in a silken swirl:
And then the painter on his canvas
    wrought,
Trying to paint the language of his
    thought.

All day the magic colors softly flowed,
  Until it seemed as if some wondrous
    spell

Possessed the hour, and like a radiance
    glowed
  In the fair lines that on his canvas
    fell:
And as the hours, down-shod, went
    slipping past,
His dream of fame seemed blossoming
    at last.

See how the witchery of that old dress
  Makes a soft mirror of the canvas,
    where,
The artist, with a lover's tenderness,
  Bestows faint glints of lustre here and
    there!
Almost to his quick fancy the folds
    stir
With their old scents of rosemary and
    myrrh!

Just then the weary girl forgetful grew
  And swept a hand along each flowing
    line,

Alas, a hundred ripples straightway flew
  In answer to that little heedless sign!
The glistening folds were changed from
    belt to hem,
All the familiar grace gone out of them.

The startled girl looked in the artist's
    face
  And read the story of his loss and
    pain.
She could not call the lines back to
    their place,
  Regret and sighing were alike in
    vain.
Naught can revive an inspiration dead;
The golden vision had forever fled!

What lesson, O my soul, is here for
    thee
  That chideth this poor model over-
    much?
To stand henceforth more still and
    patiently

Beneath the fashioning of God's fine
    touch!
For ah, what grace by the Great Artist
    planned
Has been effaced by thy impatient
    hand!

ADIEU, kind Life, though thou
    hast often been
    Lavish of quip, and scant of
    courtesy,
Beneath thy roughness I have found in
    thee
A host who doth my parting favor
    win.
Friend, teacher, sage, and sometimes
    harlequin,
Thine every mood hath held some good
    for me, —
Nor ever friendlier seemed thy company
Than on this night when I must quit
    thine inn.

4

I love thee, Life, in spite of thy rude
    ways!
  Dear is thy pleasant house, so long
    my home.
I thank thee for the hospitable days,
  The friends, the rugged cheer. Then,
    landlord, come!
Pour me a stirrup cup,— our parting
    nears;
I ever liked thy wine, though salt with
    tears.

UNSEEN GUESTS.

W E have come back — the absent
whom you miss —
To pledge with you before the
feast is done :
You do not feel our tender clasp and
kiss,
Nor hear us softly enter one by one.
Your voices drown our signals faint and
low,
But pledge your unseen guests before
you go.

We waft our souls to you as thistle-
blooms
Launch on the winds their airy mariners, —
O Hearts ! Spread wide for us your
pleasant rooms,

Nor coldly greet the eager travellers!
From your fair loving cup a draught
      bestow
On friends of " auld lang syne," before
      you go.

Our memory spells the very flowers you
      wear, —
The roses in their crystal chalices!
She knows the tricks of speech, of eyes,
      of hair: —
Ah! 't is a faithful tapestry she weaves!
And since so fair and true her colors
      show,
Then fill to Memory before you go.

And who can tell?   Perhaps they too
      are here, —
Our angels whom we wrongly name our
      dead!
Leaving their bliss awhile to linger near
Some heart that joy hath left unten-
      anted.

Ah, friends! They may be nearer than
    we know,
Then pledge them tenderly before you
    go!

Why do we call them dead from whose
    hot grasp
God kindly takes a tear-embittered bowl,
And sets instead within the longing
    clasp
His perfect cup of rapture? Nay, sad
    soul!
Name not God's richest gift to mortals so,
But quaff to Life, full Life, before you
    go!

Love is the pilot of our silent crew;
No boat so stanch, no sails so trim and
    white.
Full well he knew the path that led to
    you
Through trackless air, and sea, and
    moonless night.

Nor aught cares he how wild the March
    winds blow!
Then fill a glass to Love before you
    go.

Good-bye! Good-bye! though Love
    hath many ports
Where winds are soft and ships may lie
    at rest,
Home is the sheltered bay he fondliest
    courts, —
Home is the little harbor he loves best.
Hither we sail away, — yo ho! yo ho!
Then drain the glass to Home before
    you go.

THREESCORE AND TEN.

I AM past my threescore years
    and ten;
   I have quaffed full cups of
    bliss and bane;
Grown drunk on folly like other men,
  With its present sweet and after-pain;
I have had my share of cloud and sun;
And what is it all, when all is done?

We have had our frolic, Life and I;
  Jovial comrades we used to be.
Full sails to-day, with a silver sky,
  Anon dead calm and a sullen sea.
Now I fear the waves, so I hug the
    shore
With my tattered sail and broken oar.

I have worn love's flower upon my breast,
  And said my prayers to a woman's
    face.
The saints forgive us! If men addressed
  Such orisons to the heavenly Grace,
They would upward mount, as strong
    birds do,
And answer bring from the heavenly
    blue!

I have known the best that life can hold
  Of fame and fortune, love and power.
And when my riotous blood grew cold,
  I cheered with books the lingering
    hour;
Banqueting on the costly wine
Which Genius pours from her flagons
    fine.

Yet I would rather lie to-day
  Where orchard blooms drift down
    their snow,
And feel lost youth in my pulses play,

Its rosy wine in my hot cheeks glow;
I would rather be young, — and foolish,
forsooth, —
Than own the baubles we buy with
youth.

I would barter fortune, fame, and power,
All knowledge gained of books and
men,
For my old delight at the first spring
flower,
A robin's egg, or a captured wren
From its nest hid under the tossing
plume
Of a sweet, old-fashioned lilac bloom.

With the world's stale feast I am sur-
feited;
I long to-day for the old-time thrill
At the purple pomp of a pansy bed,
Or the fresh spring scent of a daffodil.
Alas, I shall never be thrilled again!
I am old, — yes, past threescore and ten.

A MARCH WEDDING.

IMPATIENT lovers, have you
then no care
That summer holds a month
divinely fair;
When laughing brooks and softly whis-
pering trees
Chime with the tune of birds and hum
of bees;
When color, light, and perfume everywhere,
Toss out their sumptuous banners to
the air?
Wait, then, for June, and pin the bridal
veil
With hyacinths and lilies sweet and
pale.

And yet, what matter how the March
    winds blow?
You make your own fair summer as
    you go;
Love hath, like death, all seasons for
    her own,
And in each month sets up her rosy
    throne.
And I, — worn, weary, and oppressed
    with care,
The dust of travel white upon my
    hair, —
Would give the listless years now left
    to me
For one swift moment of your ecstasy!

A GIFT OF GENTIANS.

E timid, fluttering things, whose
fringes rare ·
Are dipped in colors drawn
from babies' eyes ;
Whose robe of gossamer is spun of air,
In the same loom with June's deli-
cious skies ;
Whose dainty hems, and skirts so silken
fine,
The fairies trust no awkward brush to
trace;
Much do I marvel that, with added line,
A mortal's hand can paint each flower-
face!
But know you not the one who sought
you out

Holds in his palm such magic strong
and fine
That it has even wrapped thy grace
about
With something more delightful and
divine?
And so, with glad obeisance, do I greet
Our first acquaintance,— tender, blue-
eyed things!
For with a benediction good and sweet,
You fold within my hands your
feathery wings.
And from this day your azure wells
shall be
The mirror of a face so true and
good,
Your sweet suggestions can but be to
me
The impulse to a better womanhood!

HIS BIRTHDAY.

THE day the Christ-child's tender
eyes
Unveiled their beauty on the
earth,
God lit a new star in the skies
To flash the message of his birth;
And wise men read the glowing sign,
And came to greet the Child divine.

Low kneeling in the stable's gloom
Their precious treasures they un-
rolled;
The place was rich with sweet perfume;
Upon the floor lay gifts of gold.
And thus, adoring, they did bring
To Christ the earliest offering.

I think no nimbus wreathed the head
   Of the young King so rudely throned;
The quilt of hay beneath him spread
   The sleepy kine beside him owned;
And here and there in the torn thatch
The sky thrust in a starry patch.

Oh, when was new-born monarch
    shrined
   Within such canopy as this?
The birds have cradles feather-lined;
   And for their new babes princesses
Have sheets of lace without a flaw, —
His pillow was a wisp of straw!

He chose this way, it may have been,
   That those poor mothers, everywhere,
Whose babies in the world's great inn
   Find scanty cradle-room and fare,
As did the babe of Bethlehem,
May find somewhat to comfort them.

Thus was he born.   And since that time
  We crown the day with wreath and
    song;
The bells laugh out in merry chime,
  And he his royal Guest doth wrong
Who welcomes him with gloomy fears,
Or salts the birthday feast with tears.

COMING HOME.

I HAVE come to the dear old threshold,
   With eager, hurrying feet,
To scent the odorous lilies
   That once were so white and sweet.
To taste the apricots mellow
   That crimson the garden wall;
To gather the golden pippins
   That down in the orchard fall.

I passed by the uncut hedges,
   And up through the thistled walk,
And beside the fall of my footsteps
   There was only the crickets' talk.
The weeds grew high in the arbor,
   And the nettles, rank and tall,
Had throttled the sweet-breathed lilies
   That leaned on the latticed wall.

The little white house is empty,
  Its ceilings are cobwebbed o'er,
And the dust and mould are lying
  Thick on the trackless floor.
There are no prints in the doorway,
  No garments hung in the hall,
And the ghosts of death and silence
  Sit and gloat over all!

No eager faces of children
  Brightened the window-pane,
Never a peal of laughter
  Rippled along the lane;
So I turned through the daisies yellow,
  That nodded to see me pass,
To seek for the mellow pippins
  That drop in the orchard grass.

But I found a worm in my apples,
  And flung them sadly away;
The pool that I thought eternal
  All foul and poisonous lay.

A black snake crept from its hiding
And hissed in the marshes wild,
And I bent my head in the rushes
And sobbed like a homesick child!

A THANKSGIVING PRAYER.

OR toil that is a medicine for
    woe,
    For strength that grows with
every lifted cross,
For thorns, since with each thorn a rose
    did grow,
    For gain that I have wrongly reck-
oned loss,
For ignorance, where it were harm to
    know, —
    Teach me to thank thee, Lord.

For cups of honeyed pleasure thou
    didst spill
    Before their foam had quenched my
    purer sense;
For that my soul has power to struggle
    still,

Though panting in the trappings of
pretence;
And for mistakes that saved from
greater ill, —
Teach me to thank thee, Lord.

That thou dost ravel out the tinselled
thread
Of my poor work I thought so bravely
done;
That thou dost show me every flimsy
shred
In the thin coat of honor I have
spun,
And pluck'st the slender garland from
my head, —
Teach me to thank thee, Lord.

For ills averted, all unseen by me,
For darkened days that healed my
dazzled eyes,
For suffering which brought a company

Of gentle ministers, in stern disguise;
For weariness, which made me lean on
      thee, —
   Teach me to thank thee, Lord.

For chalices of tears that thou dost
      pour,
   For unrequited love and wounded
      pride;
If they but tempt my lonesome heart
      the more
   To seek the faithful shelter of thy
      side;
For homelessness, which drives me to
      thy door, —
   Teach me to thank thee, Lord.

OILING among my garden
thorns one day,
While in a stirless swoon the
hot air lay,
A traveller passed toward the glowing
west,
Who seemed intent upon some cheerful quest,
For with a song he did beguile the way.
Perhaps some question stirred within
my eyes,
For thus he spake: "In yonder valley
lies,
Among the murmurous trees, the Inn
called *Rest;*
Where all the pillows are with poppies
strewn,
Where toil-worn feet are shod with
silken shoon,

And bed of down awaits each jaded
  guest;
I haste at this good Inn to make request,
 For see! the dial marks the hour of
  noon."
 "God grant," I cried, "you reach
  that threshold soon!"

The singer passed, and in the winding
  lane
I lost at length the thread of his
  refrain.
 One Sabbath eve, consoled and com-
  forted
 By chant and prayer at vesper-service
  said,
With a *Laus Deo* thrilling through my
  pain,
 I left the church, and careless where
  I went,
 Behind its ivied walls my footsteps
  bent,
Among the low green tents where dwell
  the dead.

The chill winds sobbed among the
grasses sere
Which thatched the narrow roofs.
The sky was drear,
And drops of rain fell on my down-bent
head.
Turning to go, upon a stone I read
A name, and dropped upon these
words a tear:
"He sought an Inn of Rest, and
found it — here."

A STRADIVARIUS VIOLIN.

THE music of this ancient violin
Is haunted as men's chambers
sometimes are.
Along the liquid ladder of each bar
Phantoms of pleasure dance; Regret
steals in,
With happier ghosts, and Fate her
wheel doth spin.
Torn butterflies of hope a breath did
mar
Here flutter, like the flame within a star.
And if thou wouldst, O soul, nepenthe
win,
Pause not beside this portal, lest thou
hear
The voice of thy dead sorrow whis-
pering near!

For every passion that thy life hath
    known, —
Anguish benumbed, and love thou
    thought'st flown, —
Among these peerless octaves veilèd,
    wait
To speak to thee across the stringèd
    gate.

AN OCTOBER BANQUET.

ITH many a curve of her brown
    wrist,
    The hospitable vine,
In clustered bowls of amethyst,
  Hands down her unpressed wine.

A gentle courtesy is hers ;
  She works her guests no ill;
The simple goblet she confers
  Imparts no fever-thrill.

I fling the drained and broken cups
  Among the garden trees ;
While butterfly comes down and sups
  Upon the honeyed lees.

TRUST.

WITHIN the slender chalice of
    thy hand
    Hold fast what I give thee;
.   and drop down, too,
The fringes of those tender flowers
    of blue, —
Thy wondering eyes, — nor question
    nor withstand
What I may give. Perhaps my love
    hath planned
Some sweet surprise, or test if love
    be true.
What if it be a sprig of bitterest rue,
A swift, strange summons to an un-
    known land,
A hurting thorn, a cross? Strange
    gifts, 1 know,

For love to bring ; but wouldst thou
　　trust me still?
Quick, dear, — thine answer!

　　　　　　　" I should trust until
The hidden meaning in thy gift should
　　show."
Ah, sweet! when God sends just
　　such gifts to thee
Canst thou not answer him as thou
　　dost me?

THE PERFECT NICHE.

IKE some rare structure seen
    but in our dreams,
And builded of aerial warp
    and woof,
Milan Cathedral to my vision seems,
  With its fair towers and transcendent
    roof.

I see it now as on that perfect day,
  When last I climbed to where its
    glistening spires,
Like a great field of sculptured lilies
    lay,
  Fadeless and bright beneath the
    noonday fires.

Through the rich fretwork the Italian
    sky
  Thrusts its fine color, like an azure
    flower;
And in the silent night the stars on high
  Hang their soft lamps within each
    slender tower.

And niched away within the airy loft,
  Where the bell's clamor wounds the
    quiet air,
And the world's noises grow subdued
    and soft
  When they have climbed to the white
    chambers there, —

Within an arch, enriched with chiselled
    lace,
  Is a pure image, by Canova wrought,
Where none may mount its snowy lines
    to trace,
  Or read the graceful language of his
    thought.

Art may not slake her eager, burning
gaze
Beside this frozen fountain of delight;
Nor golden hammer break the carven
vase
That hides the costly incense from
our sight.

Like one white petal of a perfect bloom,
Enfolded where no human eye can see,
Canova's statue stands through sun and
gloom,
And makes its shrine a snowy har-
mony.

O life, my life! that cravest larger
place,
Prating of rusted gifts, of pinioned
feet,
Peace! — thou wilt need thine own and
borrowed grace,
If thou wouldst make thy narrow
niche complete.

CHRIST HAS RISEN!

sad-faced mourners, who each
day are wending
Through churchyard paths of
cypress and of yew,
Leave, for to-day, the low graves you
are tending,
And lift your eyes to God's eternal
blue!

Leave, for to-day, all murmuring and
sadness ;
Twine Easter lilies, and not aspho-
dels ;
Let your souls answer to the thrill of
gladness,
And to the melody of Easter bells.

If Christ were still within the grave's
    low prison, —
A captive to the enemy you dread;
If from that mouldering cell he had not
    risen,
    Who then could chide the bitter tears
    you shed?

Poor hearts! the butterfly, with pinions
    golden,
    Spurns the gray cell which erst its
    freedom barred;
And the freed soul, with wings no
    longer holden,
    Smiles back on life as on a broken
    shard.

If Christ were dead, you would have
    need to sorrow;
    But he has risen, and conquered
    death for aye!
Then dry your tears, if only till the
    morrow;
    Arise, and give your grief a holiday!

"BEHOLD, I STAND AT THE DOOR."

HEAR thy knock, O Lord,
    but, woe is me!
I have been busy in the
    world's great mart,
And have no table spread within my
    heart,
Nor any room made beautiful for thee
With burnished lamp and sprigs of
    rosemary;
And should thy stainless hands the
    curtains part,
Thy tender eyes would miss the
    joyous start, —
The happy tears, the reverent ecstasy.

Neglected is the house thy love doth
　　lend;
The ashes of dead fires bestrew the
　　hearth;
And still I hear thy voice. O Heavenly
　　Friend,
Come down to sup with me upon the
　　earth,
What if at last thou shouldst the slight
　　repay,
And welcome me as I do thee to-day?

DEAD BIRDS AND EASTER.

T was an Easter morning, bright
 and calm,
 And life, not death, was the
 glad theme that day;
The air was full of spring's delicious
 balm ;
 The maple buds were drooping on
 the way ;
And one sweet leaf, with flush of crimson on it,
Fell on the dead birds of a woman's
 bonnet.

What say the bells at these good Easter
 times?
 They tell of vanquished death and
 risen life.

Hush, then, O bells, your inconsistent
 chimes,
 You and the dull old world are hard
 at strife ;
For surely, when the crimson leaf fell
 on it,
I saw dead birds upon a woman's
 bonnet !

What does it cost, — this garniture of
 death ?
 It costs the life which God alone can
 give ;
 It costs dull silence where was music's
 breath ;
 It costs dead joy, that foolish pride
 may live.
Ah, life, and joy, and song — depend
 upon it —
Are costly trimmings for a woman's
 bonnet !

Oh, who would stop the sweet pulse of
    a lark,
  That flutters in such ecstacy of bliss,
Or lay a robin's bright breast cold and
    stark,
  For such a paltry recompense as this?
Oh, you who love your babies, think
    upon it, —
Mothers are slaughtered, just to trim
    your bonnet!

Will Herod never cease to rule the
    land,
  That we must slay sweet innocency
    so?
Is joy so cheap, or happiness sure
    planned?
  Tell me, O friend, who art acquaint
    with woe!
Does thy sad heart proclaim no protest
    on it?
Wouldst *thou* slay happiness, just for a
    bonnet?

And must God's choirs that through his
    forests rove,
Granting sweet *matinées* to high and
    low,
Must his own orchestra of field and
    grove —
    Himself their leader — be disbanded
    so?
Nay, nay! O God, proclaim thy ban
    upon it, —
Guard thy dear birds from sport, and
    greed, and bonnet!

Their fine-spun hammocks, swinging in
    the breeze,
    Should be as safe as babies' cradles
    are;
And no rude hand that tears them
    from the trees,
    Or dares a sweet bird's property
    to mar,

Deserves a woman's touch or kiss
·   upon it,
Unless — she wears dead birds upon .
her bonnet!

Dead   birds!   and dead for gentle
woman's sake,
To feed awhile her vanity's poor
breath ;
And yet the foolish bells sweet clamor
make
And tell of One whose power hath vanquished death!
Ah, Easter-time has a reproach upon it
While birds are slain to trim a woman's
bonnet!

PURPLE ASTER.

RAVELY my sweet flower resists
   Heat of August, autumn cold;
   And though she has amethysts
For her dower, and some gold,
Never roadside beggar passed her
Without nod from purple aster.

Dear plebeian, but for thee
   And thy lover, golden-rod,
Lonesomer the road would be
   Which the country folk must plod;
And each little maid and master
Would regret thee, purple aster!

When November winds blow chill,
   And the fields are brown and sear,
You will find her, cheerful still,
   With her lover standing near,
While old Winter fast and faster
Comes to claim brave purple aster.

AURORA BOREALIS.

THE northern cheek of the
    heavens,
  By a sudden glory kissed,
Blushed to the tint of roses,
  And hid in an amber mist,
And through the northern pathway,
  Trailing her robe of flame,
The queenly Borealis
  In her dazzling beauty came!

I stood and watched the tilting
  Of each dainty, rosy lance,
As it seemed to pierce the bosom
  Of an emerald expanse;
And I thought if heaven's gateway
  Is so very fair to see,
What must the inner glory
  Of the " many mansions " be?

I thought of the " Golden City,"
Where the wondrous lights unfurl;
Of its sea of clearest crystal,
Of its gates, — each one a pearl;
Thought, till the glowing splendor
Had quietly passed us by,
And the track of Aurora's chariot
Bleached out from the northern sky!

MEXICO.

ITHIN thy blue-domed Garden
of Delight,
Dwells the elusive Spirit of
Content,
And makes thy people's lot benefi-
cent.
With thee her wings forget their trick
of flight,
And brood above thy dwellers day and
night.
For thee Euterpe brings her blandish-
ment,
And Beauty hath her cornucopia spent.
Thy winds are sheathed with velvet, and
their might
Is tempered to the little naked child.

God made thee for the old and shelter-
less,
And bids fair Nature hide her moods
morose.
Thy patios with violets are tiled,
The air enfolds thee in its warm caress,
And Summer never bids thee *adios!*

WEAKNESS.

WHAT ills escape upon the world
   to-day
   Through the loose meshes of
a pliant will!
Weakness is an ignoble mistress; still,
While Passion may with bolder weapons
   slay,
Insidious Weakness doth hold equal
   sway, —
   For with such drugs she does men's
   senses fill,
   They sleep upon her knees, nor dream
   of ill;
Then Samson has the old sad price to
   pay.

From Pilate's hand she drew the sceptre
   down ;
For while he cried, "What evil hath
   He done?"
" He feared the people" and King
   Cæsar's frown
More than the anguish of the Sinless
   One,
And Weakness made him miss the
   truest fame
That ever stooped to crown a ruler's
   name !

SOME VIOLETS.

DEAR friend, I give thee violets;
    And for my fee,
The fragrant secret of thy life
Disclose to me.

For through it, like a guiding thread,
    I scent the rue,
And faintly track the odorous feet
    Of heart's-ease too.

Reach down on patient cords to me
    Thy brimming cup
Of wise, sweet thoughts, that I may
    drink,
    And thus toil up

To where thou art, so meekly high,
    So far away,
I can but kiss my eager hands
    To thee to-day.

Or, if I may not reach so high,
　　Then be it so;
If I may sit beside thy feet,
　　'T will not be low.

And, listening soft, my soul may catch
　　In some far sense
The tuneful impulse of a life
　　Serene, intense.

Ah, me! I do but spoil my work
　　With clumsy phrase;
And mar, with my uncultured speech,
　　Where I would praise.

So I will lay my heart's-ease down
　　At thy kind feet;
Regretting sore their broken stems,
　　Their vanished sweet,

Yet praying that their faded blue
　　Some type may be
Of the fair badge my heart shall wear
　　Always for thee!

WE ARE UNFAITHFUL.

IF man could rule, his love of
    change would mar
  The purple dignity that wraps
the hills;
Pluck out from the blue sky some perfect star,
  And set it elsewhere, as his fancy
  wills:

Train the gnarled apple-tree more
  straightly up ;
  Lift violet's head, so long and meekly
  bowed;
With some new odor fill her purple cup,
  And gild the rosy fringes of a cloud.

For, mark! last year I loved the violet
    best,
And tied her tender colors in my hair;
To-day I wear on my inconstant breast
    A crimson rose, and count her just as
    fair.

We are unfaithful. Only God is true
    To hold secure the landmarks of the
    past,
To paint year after year the harebell
    blue,
    And in the same sweet mould its
    shape to cast.

Oh, steadfast Nature, let us learn of
    thee!
    Thou canst create a new flower at thy
    will,
And yet through all the years canst
    faithful be
To the sweet pattern of a daffodil.

THE BURIAL OF ABRAHAM LINCOLN.*

E mourn for him whose soul on
   heights divine
   Has reached the stature of the
undefiled,
In whom a judgment ripe and honor fine
  Were blended with the nature of a
   child;
Whose pen with patient toil and godlike
   grace
   Picked out the puzzled knot of
   slavery;
Unclasped the gyves that bound a hap-
   less race,
   And dared to write "the bondman
   shall be free."

* Written by request, for the occasion of
the depositing of Abraham Lincoln's remains
in the tomb at Oak Ridge Cemetery, Spring-
field, Ill.

The kind humanities that graced his life,
The tenderness which through his
justice shone;
The sympathy that softened human
strife
And made a brother's suffering his
own;
The life which shadowed forth the per-
fect plan
Of heaven's law of equity and right:
Such were the attributes, and such the
man
Whom death has hidden from our
mortal sight.

His deeds move onward, though his life
is done;
His words still sway us like a mighty
host.
"Write down," he said, "my humble
name as one
Whose love of country was his highest
boast."

O man of men, whose name we all
    revere ! —
The dearest name in Liberty's fair
    crown ! —
Only thy corse rests in these chambers
    here ;
Death cannot touch thy honor and
    renown !

Along the years his gentle words shall
    fall, —
" With malice towards none, with
    charity for all ; "
And men shall write in tears upon his
    grave,
" He bound the nation, and unbound
    the slave."

SONG–SPARROW who had
her choice of place
The orchards over,
Espied within a bare, unsheltered space
A tuft of clover;

And here, almost beneath the passers'
feet,
Her nest confided,
While robin, with a trill of laughter
sweet,
Softly derided.

An English sparrow, curious at her
choice,
Peeped boldly under,
And cried out, in his pert plebeian
voice,
"Oh, what a blunder!"

But when the roses came, I sought the
  nest
 Of my brown sitter,
And heard, beneath her patient brood-
  ing breast,
 Young sparrows twitter.

   •

And when the withered roses strewed
  the ground,
 The fields were ringing
With the delicious and uncertain sound
 Of young birds singing.

It was the sparrows, safely fledged! and
  yet
 To human reason
That open nest, amid such dangers set,
 Seemed arrant treason.

And while these birds, serene and un-
  afraid,
 As in a tower,
Dwelt in the careless nest that they had
  made
 Beneath a flower,

A wind had rent the sturdy apple-tree,
    Where robin nested;
And from their snug, round bed her
    babies three
    Were rudely wrested.

WHITE VIOLETS.

E sought for the white violet,
　　My little love and I;
　　Among the pastures cool and
　wet,
Our feet in eager quest were set
　The dainty bloom to spy.

We knew where purple ones and blue
　Were thick as stars at night;
But all our forest journeys through
We had not found a spot where grew
　A violet of white.

Like some sweet nun, ethereal thin,
　You 'd know her anywhere,
With snowy wimple folded in
About her pale and serious chin,
　And head bent as in prayer.

In firry cloisters, spicy sweet,
　We sought our pale-faced nun.
No trace was here of her light feet;
Only a spider, trim and neat,
　Sat in the door and spun.

Where the May-apple leaves had spread
　A tent of shining green,
A moth in his gray hammock stayed,
A hermit snail sulked in the shade,
　But Violet was not seen.

The snowy star of Bethlehem
　Twinkled beside our way;
The forest's fern-embroidered hem
Glowed with red lilies, stem on stem:
　But where did Violet stay?

"Why seek white violets alone,
　My love," at last I cried,
" When　banks　with　purple　ones　are
　　strewn,
Fit for the cover of a throne,
　And coronet beside?"

" Things won," she said, " with little care
Are seldom coveted;
White violets, like pearls, are rare,
Like amethysts the purple are,
I choose the pearls," she said.

We heard the insects' drowsy croon,
Bees in the thistles slept;
The wood-thrush piped his liquid tune,
The morn led up to sultry noon,
The noon to evening crept.

We found not one white violet;
We know not where they grow.
But there are fairer treasures yet,
Sometimes, in woods and hollows wet,
As we who found them know.

IN PRISON.

OD pity the wretched prisoners,
 In their lonely cells to-day;
Whatever the sins that tripped
 them,
God pity them, still I say.

Only a strip of sunshine,
 Cleft by rusty bars;
Only a patch of azure,
 Only a cluster of stars;
Only a barren future
 To starve their hope upon;
Only stinging memories
 Of love and honor gone;
Only scorn from women,
 Only hate from men,
Only remorse to whisper
 Of a life that might have been.

Once they were little children,
  And perhaps their unstained feet
Were led by a gentle mother
  Toward the golden street;
Therefore, if in life's forest
  They since have lost their way,
For the sake of her who loved them,
  God pity them, still I say.

O mothers, gone to heaven!
  With earnest heart I ask
That your eyes may not look earthward
  On the failure of your task!
For even in those mansions
  The choking tears would rise,
Though the fairest hand in heaven
  Should wipe them from your eyes!

And you, who judge so harshly,
  Are you sure the stumbling-stone
That tripped the feet of others
  Might not have bruised your own?

Are you sure the sad-faced angel
  Who writes our errors down,
Will ascribe to you more honor
  Than to those on whom you frown?

Or, if a steadier purpose
  Unto your life is given,
A stronger will to conquer,
  A smoother path to heaven;
If, when temptations meet you,
  You crush them with a smile;
If you can chain pale passion
  And keep your lips from guile, —

Then bless the Hand that crowned you,
  Remembering, as you go,
'T was not your own endeavor
  That shaped your nature so;
And sneer not at the weakness
  Which made a brother fall,
For the hand that lifts the fallen
  God loves the best of all!

8

And pray for the wretched prisoners
  All over the land to-day,
That a holy Hand in pity
  May wipe their guilt away.

OBSCURITY.

IKE jewels hid in Ethiopian's
   breast
   The forest wears its orchids,
   and the sea
Hath richer pearls than glow in any mart;
Nature despiseth not obscurity.

She paints a world of rainbow-tinted
   things
Upon the curtains of her solitudes;
And gems the air with countless flashing
   things,
   In places where no human foot in-
   trudes.

Nor does she send her wood-thrush
   where its notes
   Will win the noisy plaudits of the
   street;

Along the leafy aisles its echoes float,
  And mingle with pine odours moist
    and sweet.

What matter that no ear the song hath
    heard?
  That no applause along the dim woods
    ran?
God needed just the music of this bird
  To round the perfect octave of His
    plan.

FOUND, within a churchyard
gray,
A marigold abloom one day,
And hotly said, " Oh, saucy elf,
Shame on thy pert and graceless self
To flaunt thy robes of yellow bloom
Among the shadows of the tomb,
And o'er the faces of the dead
To nod thy disrespectful head!
There is no fitness in thy dress,
Nor art thou modest, thus to press
Thy gaudy presence in the place
Where gladness never shows its face."

The startled flower replied: " What
claim
Hast thou to judge me? Or what shame
Should burn my cheeks because I wear
This yellow dress, which is my share
Of Nature's brightness, given to grace
The sombre shadows of this place?

I cannot harm the sleeping dead
Because I toss my golden head;
'T is all God meant for me to do,
To nod and smile the summer through.
Nor do I laugh while others weep
Through any malice, but to keep
God's perfect plan for my small life,
Unmarred by dissonance or strife;
For this I bloom beside a grave,
And wear the color that he gave."

I turned my flushing face away;
Nor will I try another day
To question any thought or plan
That God designs for flower or man.
Some lives are blithe their journey
            through,   *
While others early find the rue.
Whatever color God hath wrought
Into our life or plan or thought,
He knows the best.   There is no flaw
Nor dulness in God's perfect law!

THE NEW MESSAGE.

F ghosts of women dead a cen-
    tury
    Steal back to earth,
Then verily to-night one talked to me
    Upon my hearth.

And the pathetic minor of her tones,
    Liquid with tears,
Was like a plaintive murmur from far
    zones
    And distant years.

" Think not that I am come to you," she
    said,
    " This hallowed night
To gossip of the secrets of the dead
    Or tell their plight.

" I could not sleep; for lo! the Christ-
    mas bells
  A new tune rang:
' New birth to woman!' loud the pæan
    swells
  In rhythmic clang.

"' New birth to woman!' Once no right
    had she
  To choose her place;
Nor place had she save as man's cour-
    tesy
  Did grant her grace.

" Sometimes, by beauty, trick, or acci-
    dent,
  Grim fate she crossed;
But when from her obeisance she unbent,
  Her power was lost.

" O woman! fitly robed at last, and
    crowned
  With dignity;

Walking with lifted head your chosen
round,
Unfettered, free;

" The barbarous traditions of the past
Loosed from your feet;
Life's richest goblet held to you at last,
Brimming and sweet, —

" Forget not those for whom too late,
alas !
Dawn flushed the sky,
And to their spirits drain a silent glass.
Of such am I.

" Hark to the Christmas bells ! ' Good-
will toward men,
Peace on the earth ! '
' And unto woman ! ' — chime they forth
again —
' New birth !   New birth ! ' "

.   .   .   .   .   .

If ghosts of women dead a century
    Steal back to earth,
Then this same hour one came and
    talked to me
    Beside my hearth.

CHRISTMAS ROSES.

GAVE into a brown and tired
    hand
    A stem of roses, sweet and
creamy white.
I know the bells rang merry tunes
    that night,
For it was Christmas-time throughout
    the land,
And all the skies were hung with lan-
    terns bright.   .

The brown hand held my roses awk-
    wardly;
They seemed more white within their
    dusky vase;
The pale face glowed with pleasure
    and with praise:

"These are for daintier hands than
    mine!" cried she;
"Such beauty was not fashioned for
    my gaze."

Nay, tired one! Think, rather, that for
    you
These flowers have struggled upward
    from the clay
And journeyed on their patient, leafy
    way
Brimming their cups with light, per-
    fume, and dew,
To lay them in your palm this Christ-
    mas day.

THE genius soars far to the foun-
tain
That feeds the snow-cap in the
sky;
But though our wings break in the
flying,
And though our souls faint in the
trying,
Our flight cannot follow so high;
And the eagle swoops not from the
mountain
To answer the ground-bird's low cry.

The world has a gay guerdon ready
To hail the fleet foot in the race;
But on the dull highway of duty,
Aloof from the pomp and the
beauty,

The stir and the chance of the chase,
Are toilers, with step true and steady,
Pursuing their wearisome pace.

False prowess and noisy insistence
May capture the garrulous throng;
But the " average " father and
brother,
The home-keeping sister and
mother,
Grown gentle and patient and strong,
Shall learn in the fast-nearing distance
Wherein life's awards have been
wrong.

Then here 's to the " average " people,
The makers of home and its rest!
To them the world turns for a
blessing
When life its hard burdens is press-
ing,
For stay-at-home hearts are the best.
Birds build if they will in the steeple,
But safer the eaves for a nest.

MARCH.

I N the dark silence of her chambers low,
 March works out sweeter things
 than mortals know.

Her noiseless looms ply on with busy
 care,
Weaving the fine cloth that the flowers
 wear.

She sews the seams in violet's queer
 hood,
And paints the sweet arbutus of the
 wood.

Out of a bit of sky's delicious blue
She fashions hyacinths, and harebells
 too;

And from a sunbeam makes a cowslip
    fair,
Or spins a gown for daffodil to wear.

She pulls the cover from the crocus beds
And bids the sleepers lift their drowsy
    heads.

She marshals the close armies of the
    grass,
And polishes their green blades as they
    pass.

And all the blossoms of the fruit-trees
    sweet
Are piled in rosy shells about her feet.

Within her great alembic she distils
The dainty odor which each flower fills.

Nor does she err, and give to migno-
    nette
The perfume which belongs to violet.

Nature does well whatever task she tries,
Because obedient.   Here the secret lies.

What matter, then, that wild the March
    winds blow?
Bear patiently her lingering frost and
    snow!

For all the sweet beginnings of the
    spring
Beneath her cold brown breast lie flut-
    tering.

DISPROVED.

CANNOT think the dead come
ever back;
Else thou, my mother, wouldst
not calmly lie
Within thy grassy tent, but swiftly fly
Back through the shadowy and lonely
track
To seek the child who does thy comfort
lack.
The bliss of heaven thou wouldst thy
soul deny,
And, though so weary, all its rest
put by,
Rather than loneliness my heart should
rack.
Do souls return, my mother, and thy
kiss
Anoints not my sad eyes? Come back
and prove

How deeper than the grave is thy dear
   love !   .
Never till now didst thou the pathway
   miss
That led to me. Alas, no couriers move
From heaven to earth !   Thine ab-
   sence proveth this.

SAILING AWAY.

SAILING away from our friendly
    shores,
  Passing the cloud-ships here
    and there,
I watch the dip of your feathered oars,
  Wise little mariners of the air!

With map nor guide-book under your
    wing,
  You safely travel the azure track,
And reckon the days from fall to spring
  With never a sign of an almanac.

As I watch your flight to the summer-
    land,
  I long to sail with your merry crew;
My caged heart flutters beneath my
   ·   hand
  To try its wings in the upper blue.

But I have no chart of your sun-lit
    shores;
And my heart is heavy, it cannot fly.
Dip, dip, dip with your velvet oars;
    Happier travellers you than I!

IF I COULD CHOOSE.

WOULD not dare, though it were offered me,
  To plan my lot for but a single day,
So sure am I that all my life would be
  Marked with a blot in token of my sway.

But were it granted me this day to choose
  One shining bead from the world's jewelled string,
Favor and fortune I would quick refuse
  To grasp a richer and more costly thing.

With this brave talisman upon my breast,
  I could be ruler of my rebel soul;
To own this gem is to command the rest:
  It is the Kohinoor called Self-Control!

It is the *sesame* to broad estates,
  To peaceful slopes and mountains
    blue and fair;
Calm-browed Content beyond its border
    waits,
  And even Love sits in the sunshine
    there.

No sullen faces frown upon the street,
  No grated windows, no grim prison
    walls;
No clanking chains are bound on con-
    vict's feet,
  And on the ear no angry discord
    falls.

My life's swift river widens to the
    sea,
  The careless babble of the brook is
    past;
A few late roses blossom still for me,
  But spring is gone, and summer can-
    not last.

Had I begun with morning's rosy
    strength
To seek the flower that on life's sum-
    mit grows,
I might have found my edelweis at
    length,
And on the purple heights have
    gained repose.

But I have loitered, and the hour is late;
    Worn are my feet, and weary is my
    hand;
I can but push ajar the massive gate;
    I can but look into the Beulah land.

But, friends, if my poor love could have
    its way,
And blossom into blessing on each
    soul,
This is the very prayer that I should
    pray:
    "Grant to men's lives the power of
    self-control!"

GOOD-BY.

TO-MORROW night, when the
flush has fled
From the beautiful face of day,
And other lovers with clinging hands
Under my lattices stray;
I shall sit in the dusk alone,
And you will be far away.

Perhaps we never shall meet again
Till our burdens have been laid down,
And we have passed through the grave's
dark aisle,
With its ceilings so low and brown,
Into the warmth of the Father's smile,
Or the shadow of his frown.

And should I reach the end of the road
    Before your journey is done,
I will lean and listen beside the gate
    For the travellers, one by one;
And when I have heard your foot-fall,
      love,
    My heaven will have begun!

"MY CUP RUNNETH OVER."

JUST for to-day may I not sing
    For gratitude alone,
    Nor interrupt my praise to
    bring
Petitions to the throne?

Just for to-day may I not eat
    From yesterday's full store?
While gathered manna still is sweet,
    Shall I entreat for more?

And yet, dear Lord, I cannot live
    One hour without thy care;
So in the cup of thanks I give
    Petition, too, must share.

I am too ignorant to name
  The blessings best for me ;
The wisest prayer my lips can frame
  Is simpleness to thee.

Yet take, O God, and Friend of
    friends,
  My chalice, poor and rude,
Wherein one strong petition blends, —
  Give me more gratitude !

IN EXTREMIS.

WHILE children lean their cheeks
in drowsy prayer
Against their mother's knees,
and all the air
Is sweet with vesper bell;
See the spent day against the sunset
stand,
Her smouldering torch down-drooping
from her hand
In token of farewell.

With vague regret I watch each ebbing
grace.
Come, twilight, gentle nun, before her
face

Shall cold and ashen be;
Fold thy gray veil above her as she lies,
And sprinkle her with incense from
thine eyes:
She hath been kind to me.

THE vine upon the old church-
wall
    Has dropped its scarlet gown,
And stands, a discrowned cardinal,
    In a monk's garb of brown.

Along each maple-bordered lane,
    Which Autumn late has trod,
Her wounded feet have left a stain
    On every leaf and sod.

And here, where its own spicy scent
    Its hiding has betrayed,
Safe from the frost within the tent
    Some tattered leaves have made,

Is one belated pink as pale
   As some meek convent nun,
Whose color fades behind her veil
   For want of wind and sun.

The golden-rod, a spendthrift gay,
   Who poured for asking hands
Palms-full of gold, himself to-day
   Rusty and ragged stands!

And now, like doves with cold, gray
      breasts,
   The snow-flakes flutter by,
And brood within the empty nests
   Where young birds used to lie.

Oh, who would guess that skies so cold
   Hold in their cloaks of gray
The perfect blue and radiant gold
   Of Spring's delicious May?

N their errand of purity softly
they go,
A million fair doves from the
clouds swooping low!
They light in my window, and brood on
my sill,
With milky-white pinions down-folded
and still.

They tenderly flutter through by-way
and street,
And fold their wings over each stain
that they meet;
Until all the hedges, so ragged and
bare,
Seem dressed for a bridal resplendent
and fair.

Our little brown cottage is battered and
    worn,
Its hinges are rusty, its shutters are
    torn;
But this morning the raggedest roof in
    the town
Is shingled all over with feathers of
    down!

O doves, as you light upon meadow
    and plain
I wish you could cover man's weakness
    and stain!
Yes, I wish and I wish that the fast-
    falling snow
Could brood with its pinions our faults
    here below!

THE RAIN.

THE brooks leaped up to catch it,
　And the breezes held their
　　breath;
The lilies sprang up boldly,
　And shook their heads at death.
The roses blushed to crimson
　At the kisses of the rain;
And the sun looked out and saw it
　With a flush of jealous pain.

The thirsty little river,
　Through the faded grass that led,
Began to flash and sparkle
　Like a chain of silver thread.
It tinkled through the meadow
　Where the unraked clover lay,
Lifting its rosy blossoms,
　As the rain-king passed that way.

It left its fragrant blessing
　Along the dingy street;
It cooled the heated pavement
　For the tread of tired feet;
It stole within the chamber
　Where a sick one longed for death,
And filled the slender nostrils
　With its life-giving breath.

Upon the fluttering pulses
　It laid a wondrous calm,
And on the quivering eyelids
　It poured a slumberous balm.
It drew from the hot forehead
　The burning darts of pain,
And tired watchers slumbered,
　Lulled by its soft refrain.

A POMPEIAN PREACHER.

DEAR, dainty little " Maiden
Hair,"
Whose slender figure, trim
and. fair,
Apparelled in the softest green,
Seems fit for court of faerie queen,

I marvel much that without fear
Your tender life finds shelter here,
Where silence, death, and grim decay
Stalk like pale phantoms day by day!

No little child with dancing feet
Embroiders, by its presence sweet,
A thread of grace within the gloom
That curtains every silent room.

The sunshine, with its soft, warm feet,
Shrinks back from the unfriendly street,
And God's free light steals through the
    doors,
And shivers on the marble floors.

The timid lizard noiseless glides,
The slothful snail in calm abides;
But nothing that is fresh or fair
Dwells here save thee, dear "Maiden
    Hair!"

The place where thou dost choose to be
Was once a hall of equity;
A court, where Justice, stern and cold,
Untouched by Mercy, ruled of old.

Too delicate art thou, and fair,
To dwell in such a chilling air;
And yet, within these ruins gray,
Thou livest thy perfect life to-day.

Thou art a preacher, sweet and good,
And this low niche where thou hast
    stood,
Thy pulpit, from whose tiny walls
A sermon, quaint and earnest, falls.

O patient lives that sunless are,
From whom bright fortune stands afar!
Ye came not to your present state
By any careless chance; but Fate,

Whose name is God, hath planned it so,
With kinder forethought than we know!
And if athwart thy web of gray,
Thou runnest no brightness day by day,

Be sure thou hast not wrought so well
As this shy flower, whose name I tell, —
This dweller in Pompeian air, —
My little preacher, "Maiden Hair!"

EXPIATION.

DEATH! we call thee tyrant
in our blindness,
And yet thou showest us full
gentle ways;
And teachest far more charity and kind-
ness
Than the gay flatterer, Life, whom
most we praise!

The sword which we had bared for
angry smiting
Thou hidest in a sheath of flowers, O
Death!
And wrongs we fancied needed stern
requiting
Fade out like morning mists at thy
chaste breath.

Before some vanished friend we swing
    our censer,
And burn our candles at her empty
    shrine;
As if for past neglect to recompense
    her,
Or memory to drug with perfumes
    fine.

We wound the living heart, yet clip the
    briers
From roses that we lay in pulseless
    hands;
We build for frozen hearts our tardy
    fires,
And pour love's chalice upon grave-
    yard sands.

'T was ever thus. Men scourged the
    living Saviour,
And plaited thorns among His holy
    hair;

Then sought to expiate their mad be-
 havior
 By climbing on their knees some
  sacred stair.

Life hath one path to heights of expi-
 ation,
 Where souls stung by remorse may
  gather balm;
But by no single bound or swift trans-
 lation
 May eager pilgrims reach their purple
  calm.

The debt thou owest the dead, pay to
  the living;
 For every guilt-spot on thy memory
Drop into some sad hand that needs
  thy giving
 A shining bead from love's rich
  rosary.

Haste, if the debt be thine, for time is
    pressing !
Soon must the beads upon thy thread
    be spent,
And thou set down thy cup of dole and
    blessing
To pass within the curtain of Death's
    tent.

WHAT WILL IT MATTER?

HAT will it matter in a little
   while
   That for a day
We met and gave a word, a touch, a
   smile,
   Upon the way?

What will it matter whether hearts were
   brave,
   And lives were true;
That you gave me the sympathy I
   crave,
   As I gave you?

These trifles, — can it be they make or
   mar
   A human life?
Are souls as lightly swayed as rushes
   are,
   By love, or strife?

Yea, yea! a look the fainting heart may
break,
Or make it whole:
And just one word, if said for love's
sweet sake,
May save a soul!

YOUR BIRTHDAY.

"THIS is the day my friend was
      born to me!"
    I cried this morning with a
      thrill and start;
"O birthday bells, ring out right merrily,
    And hang your banners out, my
      happy heart!
It matters not what the storm-signals
      say, —
It is fair weather in my soul to-day!"

Not like all other days is this, O friend,
    And I would make some grateful,
      glad ado;
What signal message can I straightway
      send
    To prove I consecrate the hours to
      you?

I would salute each silent, shadowy
  mast
Of your good years as they go sailing
  past.

What have they brought to you, these
  phantom ships?
  Some silver dust, to sprinkle on the
  hair?
A faded rose, to lay upon the lips?
  Some shining tears? A green grave
  here and there?
A jagged cross? A tired brain and
  heart?
Ah, friend, are these of thy rich freight
  a part?

Or are they pirate ships whose dark
  offence
  Is stealing from us youth so fair and
  good?
The "sweet first time" of glad experience

Of hope, and dewy love, and parent-
     hood?
Is it for this their misty sails unfurl,
Just to make plunder of our gold and
     pearl?

Nay, nay! if so, more fit were funeral
     knells
  And wreaths of cypress, — one for
     each dead year, —
Than the sweet jangle of the joyous
     bells,
  The glad " God bless you! " and the
     birthday cheer.
God guides the years, and freights them
     as is best;
Let us have patience till we know the
     rest.

Ah, how like little children we are led
  Up to the threshold of the future
     years,
To every waiting sorrow blindfolded,

And all unconscious of to-morrow's
tears!
And when to-morrow comes, we find it
still
Holds just the strength sufficient for
its ill!

O gentle Trust! if to possess thy grace
Needed long journeys to some ancient
shrine,
Though faint and weary, we would seek
the place
From rosy dawn till midnight stars
should shine!
But they who find thy presence know
full well
That in no far-off country dost thou
dwell.

Oh, what can not her gentle presence
do?
It is a flower upon sick pillows
thrown;

The rose that hides the rankling thorn
 from view;
 The velvet moss upon old towers
 grown.
It is a box of ointment rare and sweet,
Which we may break upon the Holy
 feet.

And now, dear friend, I think you
 understand,
 That if to-day some happy prayer of
 mine
Could bring a white gift fluttering to
 your hand,
 I would not ask for things that flash
 and shine, —
But that upon your threshold God
 might lay
This flower of trust to crown your
 natal day.   ·

SAD, sad soul, fling wide your
    doors,
  And make your windows cur-
    tainless;
Strew odours on your silent floors,
  And all your walls with lilies dress!

Throw open every sombre place;
  Roll every hindering stone away;
Let Easter sunshine gild your face,
  And bless you with its warmth to-day!

Let friends renew each bygone hour;
  Let children fling the world a kiss;
And every hand tie in some flower,
  To crown a day so good as this!

And whether skies are sad or clear,
    We'll give the day to joy and song;
For since the Christ is surely here,
    All things are right, and naught is
      wrong!

O BELLS IN THE STEEPLE.

BELLS in the steeple,
Ring out to all people
That Christ has arisen, — that
Jesus is here !
Touch heaven's blue ceiling
With your happy pealing ;
O bells in the steeple, ring out full and
clear !

O soft April showers,
Call out the young flowers,
Touch each little sleeper, and bid her
obey ;
Set daffodils blowing,
And fresh grasses growing,
To thrill the old world on this new
Easter-day !

O lilies so stately, —
Like maids tall and shapely, —
Christ loved you, and talked of your
　　beauty of old;
Stand up in your places,
And bend your white faces,
While swinging before Him your censers
　　of gold!

O violets tender,
Your shy tribute render!
Tie round your wet faces your soft
　　hoods of blue;
And carry your sweetness,
Your dainty completeness,
To some tired hand that is longing
　　for you.

O velvet-bloomed willows,
Go comfort sick pillows
With visions of meadow-lands, peace-
　　ful and brown!

The breath of Spring lingers
Within your cold fingers,
And the brook's song is caught in your
fringes of down.

O world, bowed and broken
With anguish unspoken,
Take heart and be glad, for the Lord is
not dead!
On some bright to-morrow,
Your black cloud of sorrow
Will break in a sweet rain of joy on
your head.

O bells in the steeple,
Ring out to all people
That Christ has arisen,— that Jesus is
here!
Touch heaven's blue ceiling
With your happy pealing;
O bells in the steeple, ring out full and
clear!

IN SILENCE.

S loving friends sit sometimes
      hand in hand,
   Nor mar with sound the sweet
speech of their eyes;
So in soft silence let us oftener kneel,
   Nor try with words to make God
   understand.
Longing is prayer; upon its wings we
      rise
   To where the airs of heaven around
   us steal.

MY MOTHER.

The sweetest face in all the world to me,
  Set in a frame of shining silver hair,
With eyes whose language is fidelity :
  This is my mother. Is she not most fair ?

Ten little heads have found their sweetest rest
  Upon the pillow of her loving breast:
The world is wide ; yet nowhere does it keep
  So safe a haven, so secure a rest.

'Tis counted something great to be a queen,
  And bend a kingdom to a woman's will.
To be a mother such as mine, I ween,
  Is something better and more noble still.

O mother ! in the changeful years now flown,
Since, as a child, I leaned upon your knee,
Life has not brought to me, nor fortune shown,
Such tender love ! such yearning sympathy !

Let fortune smile or frown, whiche'er she will ;
It matters not, I scorn her fickle ways !
I never shall be quite bereft until
I lose my mother's honest blame and praise !

CONTENTS.

———◆———

Contents,

SHE CAME TO ME.

NOT with the rustle of strange
wings,
Not as an angel garmented;
No aureole shone round her head,
She did not speak of heavenly things.

She came and stood beside my knee,
Leaning upon it as of old;
Until my sorrow, fold on fold,
Like an old garment fell from me.

The very frock she used to wear,
The lace about her sweet, round wrist;
The warm moist hand that I had kissed;
The wayward trick of the bright hair.

That on her lifted forehead fell, —
  I saw it all in rapt surprise,
  As smiling upward with her eyes
She said, " I 'm all well now — all well."

O little queen, whose realm on earth
  In ruin lies ! leave not the road
  Between thy world and ours untrod ;
Come sometimes back to the old hearth !

We will not bar the chamber door,
  To hinder thy departing feet :
  We know thou canst not tarry, Sweet,
But come, O come to us once more !

THE BABY OVER THE WAY.

CROSS in my neighbor's window,
   With its folds of satin and lace,
   I see, with its crown of ringlets,
A baby's innocent face.
The throng in the street look upward,
   And every one, grave or gay,
Has a nod and a smile for the baby,
   In the mansion over the way.

Just here in my cottage window,
   His chin in his dimpled hands,
And a patch on his faded apron,
   The child that I live for stands.
He has kept my heart from breaking
   For many a weary day;
And his face is as pure and handsome
   As the baby's over the way.

Sometimes, when we sit together,
  My grave little man of three,
Sore vexes me with the question,
  "Does God up in Heaven like me?"
And I say, "Yes, yes, my darling,"
  Though I almost answer "Nay":
As I see the nursery candles,
  In the mansion over the way.

And oft when I draw the stocking
  From his little tired feet,
And loosen the clumsy garments
  From his limbs so round and sweet,
I grow too bitter for singing,
  My heart too heavy to pray,
As I think of the dainty raiment
  Of the baby over the way.

        .   .   .   .   .

Oh God in Heaven forgive me
  For all I have thought and said!
My envious heart is humbled:
  My neighbor's baby is dead!

I saw the little white coffin
  As they carried it out to-day,
And the heart of a mother's is breaking
  In the mansion over the way!

The light is fair in my window,
  The flowers bloom at my door;
My boy is chasing the sunbeams
  That dance on the cottage floor.
The roses of health are crowning
  My darling's forehead to-day;
But the baby is gone from the window
  Of the mansion over the way!

FOUR. ·

H, wind of the sweet May morning!
    Tell me the rarest thing,
    The fittest for birthday token,
  That your rosy hands can bring.
Oh, army of loving mothers,
    Lend me your counsel, pray,
And tell me a gift for a darling
  Who is four years old to-day!

I have hunted the clover meadow
  And the blossoming orchards through
For a bit of the robin's crimson,
  Or the jay-bird's dainty blue;
But robin, at home with her babies,
  Was having a holiday,
And when I made love to the blue-bird,
  She whistled and fluttered away.

I CANNOT tell
    How it befell ·
As you came sailing straight
    to me,
  That no sweet hail,
  Nor rustling sail
Proclaimed my coming argosy.

  Yet every day
  Upon its way
Your boat was speeding sure and fast;
  Until my eyes
  With glad surprise
Beheld and welcomed you at last.

  I cannot see
  How it could be
I saw no signal from your hand;
  Yet this I know,
  With happy glow,
Your boat to-day is at my strand.

2

A LITTLE PILLOW.

LITTLE pillow, do you think,
   With your frills and bows of pink,
   You can faithful be and true,
To the trust I give to you?
In your laces, here and there,
I have stitched a silent prayer
For the little child, whose face
Soon will give a needed grace
To the work my hands have wrought
With full many a tender thought.

Underneath each knot of pink
Hides a sleepy elf, I think,
Who, with tricks so sly and wise,
Fastens down the baby's eyes;
Wraps him round from brow to feet
With a rest so soft and sweet,

That he cries in grieved surprise,
When he opens wide his eyes,
Just because he cannot keep
All the treasures of his sleep!

To each feather soft and white
I have whispered dreams so light,
That the baby's sleep will be
Full of peace and purity.
What though velvet cheek and lips,
With their rosiness eclipse
Every touch of puny skill,
I have wrought with loving will?

How could anything compare
With a baby fresh and fair?
How could God's work pure and fine;
Ever harmonize with mine?
Little pillow do you think,
With your frills and bows of pink
You can faithful be and true
To the trust I give to you?

"LOST—A GIRL."

H, say! have you seen my Alice
　　Anywhere on Life's street,
　　Among the army of children
　Everywhere that you meet?
Her hair was in yellow tangles,
　There were prints of sweets on her face,
She spoke in a broken language,
　And lisped with a child's rare grace.

Has nobody seen this hoyden,
　This queer little girl in blue,
With a rent in her wee white apron
　And a gap in each scarlet shoe?
Her shoe-strings were always dangling,
　And her stockings sure to be
Loosed and showing the dimples
　Set in each rosy knee.

If angels had stolen our Alice
   Away from.her life of play;
If under a cover of daisies
   We had hidden our girl away;
If I could know she had wandered
   The Heavenly gateway through,
I should think some day to find her,
   My little daughter in blue.

The birds have learned to answer
   When her name I sadly call,
But the voice of my little truant
   Is silent, in room and hall.
I see a beautiful *woman*
   With my grandchild at her knee,
But my little heedless Alice
   Will never come back to me!

MY BABY'S MOUTH.

HE had not compassed much of
    human speech
  With that small mouth, like two
    rose-petals curled;
But the short octave that her tongue could
  reach,
  Out-sweetened all the music in the world.

Yet when my child was with me every day,
  I wore her heedlessly upon my breast,—
My tender flower! — It is our human
    way;
  We mothers are too thoughtless at the
    best.

For had some angel stooped from heaven
    to touch
  With that same tenderness my brow
    and hair,

I should have thrilled and trembled overmuch,
And set some consecrated signet there.

I seal it now, God and the angels know!
And on the strength of every slighted
kiss
I will drink humbly my full cup of woe,
Nor grudge the price for my neglected
bliss.

O world, you nothing hold that I regret:
I covet neither honors, wealth, nor place;
I want my baby's mouth all sweet and
wet,
Rubbing its dew against my lonely face!

NESTS.

I KNOW where meadow-grasses
    rank and high
    A cradle cover,
Because two bobolinks with tell-tale cry
    Above them hover.

Some mullein leaves beside my garden
    wall
    Grow unmolested;
And under their pale velvet parasol
    Sparrows have nested.

An oriole toiled on from day to day —
    The cunning weaver! —
Tying her hammock to that leafy spray
    Above the river.

No wingless thief can climb that elm's frail
    stair;   •
Nor guest unbidden
Can reach the snug, aerial chamber where
    Her eggs are hidden.

A marsh-wren's cunning hermitage I see,
    As my boat passes,
Moored to the green stems of a *fleur-de-lis*
    With strong sea grasses.

And stay! I know another pretty nest
    Of braided willow,
With dainty lace, and knots of ribbon
    drest,
    And feather pillow.

And just one bird, with moist and downy
    head,   ·
    Herein reposes;
He has no wings, — his shoulders grow
    instead
    Dimples and roses!

You have a nest and little wingless bird
. At your house, may be;
Of course you know without another
word
I mean — a baby!

THE CHILD THAT BELONGS TO ME.

O pure is my child, that I dare to
    say
        His Maker would not despise
To color the sky on some rare June day
    From the blue in his handsome eyes;
And I am as proud as mother can be
Of this beautiful boy that belongs to me!

Sometimes when we walk where the lily
    blows,
        She frowns with a sullen grace;
The gentle violet jealous grows
    When my little one breathes in her
        face;
And even the rose bends courteously
To the beautiful boy that belongs to me.

His voice is as clear and sweet as the bell
   That swings in the robin's throat;
I have asked him oft, but he cannot tell
   Wherever he caught its note;
And where is the bird more happy and
      free
Than the beautiful boy that belongs to
      me!

Whenever I go to the market-place
   I carry him proud and high,
That all may catch a glimpse of his face
   Before we have passed them by;
So eager am I that the world shall see
This beautiful boy that belongs to me!

They tell me the world is a dreary place,
   And heavily sown with tears;
But when I look in my child's dear face,
   My heart is too glad for fears;
And all I can give seems a worthless fee
For the beautiful boy that belongs to me.

Nor will I burden my days with sighs,
   Lest God for my child should send;
For whether he lives or whether he dies,
   He is mine till Eternity's end.
And I fear no harm to my child or me,
Since both, O Father, belong to Thee!

IN THE DOOR.

OR forty years this old gray sentinel
  Has braved the tempest and the driving rain ;
For forty years its rusty hinge has creaked
  To let the sunshine in and out again.

The little hands that reached to clasp the latch
  Are clean enough to-day, the angels know ;
For they were emptied of the toys of life,
  And folded passively long years ago.

I brush away the cobwebs and the dust,
  And sit me down upon the sunken sill ;
And through the gate and up the garden walk,
  I seem to see my children trooping still.

Their merry voices cheer my lonesome
　　ear;
Their little garments brush me as they
　　pass;
And all along the path their feet have
　　come
A trail of sunshine parts the bended
　　grass.

I am no longer tired, worn, and gray;
　　My children cling about me as of yore;
And with their hands clasped tightly in
　　my own,
We watch the sunset from the open
　　door.

TIRED MOTHERS.

A LITTLE elbow leans upon your knee,
  Your tired knee, that has so
    much to bear;
A child's dear eyes are looking lovingly
  From underneath a thatch of shining
    hair:
Perhaps you do not heed the velvet touch
  Of warm, moist fingers, folding yours
    so tight,
You do not prize this blessing overmuch —
  You almost are too tired to pray,
    to-night!

But it *is* blessedness! A year ago
  I did not see it as I do to-day,
We are so dull and thankless; and too
    slow
  To catch the sunshine e'er it slips away.

And now it seems surpassing strange to me,
That while I wore the badge of mother-
hood,
I did not kiss more oft and tenderly
The little child that brought me only
good!

And if some night when you sit down to
rest,
You miss this elbow from your tired
knee;
This restless, curling head from off your
breast,
This lisping tongue that chatters
constantly;
If from your own the dimpled hand had
slipped, .
And ne'er would nestle in your palm
again;
If the white feet into their grave had
tripped,
I could not blame you for your heart-
ache then!

I wonder so that mothers ever fret
  At little children, clinging to their gown;
Or that the footprints, when the days are
    wet,
  Are ever black enough to make them
    frown!
If I could find a little muddy boot,
  Or cap, or jacket, on my chamber floor;
If I could kiss a rosy, restless foot,
  And hear its music in my home once
    more;

If I could mend a broken cart to-day,
  To-morrow make a kite to reach the sky,
There is no woman in God's world could
    say
  She was more blissfully content than I.
But, ah! the dainty pillow next my own
  Is never rumpled by a shining head;
My singing birdling from its nest is flown:
  The little boy I used to kiss is dead!

THE SANTA CLAUS STORY.

HOW sweet it all was! The red
firelight,
    The cat purring soft on the rug,
The wife flitting backwards and forwards,
    The egg-nog afoam in the mug.
And when I looked up at the starlight,
    And down at this picture so fair,
I just dropped my head, and in silence
    Gave thanks to the Giver right there.

The parson came in, and we told him
    How happy our boy Fritzy was,
A-hanging his little gray stocking,
    And prattling about Santa Claus.
And how Alice said as she kissed me,
    A-reaching my neck on tip-toe:
"I tould n't hold any more dladness,
    Dear papa, unless I should drow."

But the parson sat gloomy and solemn,
  And wife looked just ready to cry
When he said, "Is it right, my good
    brother,
 To tell them that old-fashioned lie?
You can't expect roses and lilies
  ·In a garden where thistles are sown,
Nor truth from the lips of your children,
  If you let falsehood blacken your
    own."

Then he said "Merry Christmas," and
    left us,
  That dazed, and so kind of unstrung,
That we stared at those little gray
    stockings,
  Till the bells in the church steeple
    rung.
And their chimes took me back to my
    mother,
  And I stood a wee chap at her knee,
And heard the same Santa Claus story
  That Mary and Fritz have, from me.

And if the Lord reckons it sinful
I hope He will punish it light:
Just think what a world full of sinners
Have told that old story to-night!

COMPENSATION.

HE folded up the worn and mended frock
   And smoothed it tenderly upon her knee,
Then through the soft web of a wee red sock
   She wove the bright wool, musing thoughtfully,
"Can this be all? The great world is so fair,
   I hunger for its green and pleasant ways;
A cripple prisoned in her restless chair,
   Looks from her window with a wistful gaze.

"The fruits I cannot reach are red and sweet,
   The paths forbidden are both green and wide;

O God! there is no boon to helpless feet
So altogether sweet as paths denied.
Home is most fair: bright are my
household fires,
And children are a gift without alloy:
But who would bound the field of her
desires
By the prim hedges of mere fireside
joy?

"I can but weave a faint thread to and
fro,
Making a frail woof in a baby's sock;
Into the world's sweet tumult I would go,
At its strong gates my trembling hand
would knock."
Just then the children came, the father
too,
Their eager faces lit the twilight gloom,
"Dear heart," he whispered, as he nearer
drew,
"How sweet it is within this little
room!

" God puts my strongest comfort here to
    draw
  When thirst is great, and common wells
    are dry.
Your pure desire is my unerring law;
  Tell me, dear one, who is so safe as I?
Home is the pasture where my soul may
    feed,
  This room a paradise has grown to be,
And only where these patient feet shall
    lead
  Can it be home for these dear ones and
    me."

He touched with reverent hand the
    helpless feet,
  The children crowded close and kissed
    her hair.
" Our mother is so good, and kind, and
    sweet,
  There's not another like her anywhere ! "
The baby in her low bed opened wide
  The soft blue flowers of her timid eyes,

And viewed the group about the cradle
   side
With smiles of glad and innocent
   surprise.

The mother drew the baby to her breast
   And smiling said: "The stars shine
   soft to-night;
My world is fair; its hedges, too, are best
And whatsoever is, dear Lord, is right."

TWO VALENTINES.

NE was the loveliest thing! A
  pink sachet
  Trimmed with soft ribbons and
  point appliqué,
While heliotropes upon their rosy field
The daintiest of perfumes seemed to
  yield.

Tom thought it just the thing, and then he
  knew
The nicest girl in town would think so
  too;
And, best of all, within the folds was laid
A valentine to please the little maid:

"What is daintier, can you tell,
Than the lichen groves where the fairies
  dwell?

What is a still more delicate thing
Than the silken stuff of a butterfly's
    wing?
What has a lining do you think
As fair as the mushroom's fluted pink?

"Are you so dull?   Why, the rarest
        thing
Is the heart of the girl whose praise I
    sing!"

This he addressed to Miss Maude Alice
    Browne.
Another — how I blush to write it down —
He sent in spite to poor lame Meg
    McCray,
Who won the prize in algebra that day.

"There is a young person I know,
Whose shoes are all out at the toe ;
        She has very large feet,
        Her gown is not neat,
And her petticoats hang down below.

"I *may* ride a broom to the sky,
A snow-storm *may* fall in July,
    And my slatternly friend
    Her habits *may* mend ;
But do you believe it?   Not I."

But can you tell me how it came about
That Miss Maude Alice Browne, with
        laugh and shout,
Received Meg's valentine?   And, strange
        to tell,
Miss Meg McCray received Miss Browne's
        as well.

"O Tom!" Meg cried with innocent,
        round eyes,
"I 've had the dearest kind of a sur-
        prise!
Now who could love a poor, lame girl
        like me
Enough to send this valentine?   Just
        see!

"If I were rich like Miss Maude Alice
 Browne,
And pretty, too— Why, Tom, what makes
 you frown? —
It could not be so sweet to me, you know,
To feel that some kind person loves me
 so.

"But now whenever things seem hard to
 bear,
I think it will be easier not to care,
And being lame will not seem quite so
 bad,
The thought that some one cares makes
 me so glad.

Tom looked perplexed. What could the
 fellow do
But say, " Well, Meg, I'm just as glad as
 you!"
And so he was: the jealous fiend had
 flown
And in his eyes a true repentance shone.

And Miss Maude Alice Brown cried with
    a laugh,
"Some one has sent me my own photo-
    graph!
Well it's a joke, and here's the best of it,
It does n't hurt because it does n't hit!"

That night Tom's sister touched him on
    the knee:
" I say, dear Tom," she said michievously,
" I wonder if the Lord will credit you
With what you *did*, or what you *meant* to
    do."

JOE'S MERCIES.

Well, I 've been counting my mercies,
  As my grandmother would say,
And I have n't got many to brag of,
  If it is Thanksgiving Day.

There 's mother, of course, and the baby,
  They 're down in big letters, you know,
But between you and me, the remainder
  Don't make an exceeding long row.

For grandma is very uncertain,
  And likely as not, before long,
To quietly slip off and leave us —
  She is seventy, and not very strong.

And I would n't give a brass button
  For a palace, no matter how fine,
That has n't a grandmother in it
  That looks pretty nearly like mine.

And then, you will own, it's a trial,
　To be so exceedingly poor;
It takes just a few extra mercies
　To make up for that, I am sure.

To-day, we'll have beef and rice pudding,
　Thanksgiving at that.　What a feast!
One ought to expect a plump turkey
　And cranberry sauce, at least.

And you can't guess how lonesome it is
　　　Jack,
　For a shaver no bigger than I,
To manage without any father,
　And I hope that you won't have to try.

And the more I try to be thankful
　And think of my blessings and such;
The more it appears, on that subject,
　What I have to say is not much.

And as for the weather — it's horrid!
　Just look at the frost on the glass!
Why, I couldn't catch sight of a circus
　If one should happen to pass.

Say, Jacky just come to the window;
  What is it on Benny Bright's door?
It 's a strip of white crape and a ribbon !
  O Jack, had you seen it before?

And there goes a little white coffin
  And flowers.   Yes, Jack, now I see !
It is Ben's little rosy-faced brother,
  Who always threw kisses at me.

Oh, I am the worst of boys, Jacky,
  Don't any one dare tell me " No,"
I tell you I 'll whip the first fellow
  That offers to say it ain't so.

But, Jack, it never once struck me
  Till I saw that small coffin, to-day,
How much a little round baby,
  Like the one at our house, can weigh.

But I say, if in counting his mercies
  A boy is inclined to be slow,
A hearse at the door of his neighbor
  Will quicken his senses, I know.

4

At any rate that's my opinion;
   And I think, if the Lord does n't care,
I 'll reckon my mercies all over;
   For, Jacky, I did n't count fair.

MY LITTLE BOY.

THE old square clock had struck
the hour of eight.
Outside the starry lamps were
shining high,
The silver moon in regal splendor sate
In the blue glory of the Christmas sky,
And tired workers toiling homeward late
Hummed Christmas carols as they
plodded by.

My little boy was standing by my chair,
One small white foot was bare upon the
floor;
His shining eyes beheld a world all fair;
His face was eloquent with hopes in
store,
For hanging in the chimney corner there
Was the small fleecy sock my darling
wore.

He had been telling me in eager speech
  Of all the treasures Santa Claus would
      bring;
There were no bounds his sweet faith
      could not reach,
  His trust was simple and unquestion-
      ing,
While I had learned the whole that life
      could teach
  Of bitter doubt and cruel suffering!

I listened to him with a wistful prayer,
  I longed to make some helpful faith my
      own;
That into my poor life of grief and
      care
  Might creep a truer grace than it had
      known —
Some blessed trust that would not prove a
      snare,
  Some love more honest than the world
      had shown.

And then I said, " The Christmas is to me
  More sad, my boy, than you can
    understand;
It brings me gifts of pain and treachery,
  And deals them through a loved and
    trusted hand.
It brings a broken truth my staff to be,
  And leaves me nothing that will hold or
    stand!

My blessed child broke in upon my woe,
  Half loving, half reproachfully he said,
" You still have something left; there 's
    me, you know!
  Why, one might think your little boy
    was dead!
I 'm little now, but when I larger grow
  I will take care of you, mamma," he
    said.

I caught him with a passionate surprise;
  I covered him with kisses burning
    sweet!

My life grew richer, looking in his eyes,
   Though other loves were poor and
      incomplete ;
And praying God to make him good and
      wise,
   I tucked the cover soft about his feet.

WHAT CAN I DO?

WHAT can I do, O heavy heart
within,
That shall atone
For this most sacrilegious sin
That I have done?

For when my soul would seek the King
alone
A round bright head
Lifts up its aureole before the throne
And shines instead.

Nor gates of pearl, nor walls of amethyst
That flash and glow,
Have grace and color like the eyes I
kissed
A year ago.

And Christ forgive me! All the bliss and
   balm
   Of that rare land
Are held, for me, within the slender palm
Of one small hand!

One day my soul may climb on holier
   round
   To Heaven's fair place:
But now, ah me! my fierce desire is
   bound
   By one sweet face.

WHO HATH MADE THEM TO DIFFER.

HO hath made them to differ —
Your little child and mine?
Each with a face like the flower,
Each with the stamp divine!
Who hath made them to differ —
The lamb in the sheltering fold,
And the waif with never a pasture,
Bleating for hunger and cold?

Is it God that wrought the evil?
Does He fashion the tender flower
Only to trample its chalice
Under the tread of His power?
Is it God, the Father of Mercies,
The Blameless, the Undefiled,
Who hath wrought this pitiful evil
In the life of a little child?

Hath He erred somehow like a mortal,
That the children cry for bread?
Is it God hath failed in His weaving
And twisted and soiled the thread?
Nay, nay, He is just, and our Father,
He cannot beget a wrong!
We clash the keys of His organ
And then blame Him for the song.

We thrust our hands in His purpose,
And tangle them in His wheel,
And then cry out like children,
For the hurt we needs must feel.
We shatter our cup of blessing,
Its portion we waste or spill,
And then complain and wonder
That the poor are hungry still.

When wast Thou sick, O Saviour!
And I ministered not to Thee?
" If thou didst it not to my brother
Thou didst it not unto me."

Then haste while the pool is troubled!
Haste in the name of Him!
And lift with the clasp of a mother
Some sufferer over the brim!

PAPA'S BIRTHDAY.

WHAT *is* a birthday, papa?
　　Is it something nice for you?
　　Are they good for little fellows?
And can *I* have one, too?
This world is full of puzzles
　　To bother boys about;
But it's a pretty hard one
　　My papa can't make out.

Mamma says love is fairest
　　Of all the gifts we bring;
A *very* great deal sweeter
　　Than any other thing.
Then, if there's nothing better,
　　And mamma tells me true,
Oh, take it for your birthday
　　From your little boy to you!

THE LOST CHRISTMAS.

HE Russian peasants tell to-day
　　A legend old and dear to them,
How, when the wise men went
　　their way
　　To find the Babe at Bethlehem,

They paused to let their camels rest
　　Beside a peasant's lowly door;
And all intent upon their quest
　　They talked their sacred errand o'er.

"Come with us," said the eager three;
　　"Come, seek with us the heavenly Child;
What prouder honor can there be
　　For mortals, sinful and defiled?

"And bid each child in Sunday clothes
  Bring of his treasures the most rare,
Bundles of myrrh and whitest doves,
    With ointment for the Christ-King's
    hair.

"Who knows what blessing may befall
  If they but touch His garment's hem?
And only once for them and all
    Will Christ be born at Bethlehem!"

"Alas! My task must first be done,"
  The mother answered with a sigh;
"But I would see the holy one,
  And I will follow by and by."

The wise men frowned and onward went,
  Leaving the children all aglow,
And pleading till the day was spent,
  "When may we go? When may we
    go?"

And while their cheeks flushed rosy red,
　They shouted in a chorus sweet:
" And may we touch His pretty head?
　And may we kiss His blessed feet?"

But women still will brew and bake,
　No matter what sweet honors wait;
And petty tasks they undertake,
　Though angels tarry at the gate!

And when all things were in their place,
　And every child was neat and trim;
When each tear-stained and tired face
　Was bathed and tied its hood within;

The sky was purpling in the west,
　The silent night was hurrying on;
The three wise men had onward pressed,
　The star from out the east had gone!

What could the foolish mother do?
　She turned her footsteps home again;
And never, all her sad life through,
　Did she behold the three wise men.

And thus through weak delaying she
　Her sweetest privilege had missed;
Nor ever did her children see
　The Holy Babe they might have kissed.

A SWEET OLD LEGEND.

BRING that low footstool from the
    corner, Ted;
    Mary and Jack you cannot crowd
    too near;
While baby Bess will curl her pretty
    head
Against my heart, that holds you all so
    dear.

Now for the legend. Once, long years
    ago,
When in our world the blessed Lord
    was seen,
He walked one evening, tired, sad, and
    slow,
With His disciples through the meadows
    green.

5

Why was He sad? Dear child, I cannot
    say
What burdens pressed upon His heart
    divine —
Perhaps none had believed on Him that
    day;
    Perhaps He thought upon your sins
    and mine.

Along the way the sweet field lilies grew
    In rich apparel, finer than a king's;
Above His head the twittering sparrows
    flew —
    (He drew His sermons from these
    simple things).

Now as they walked on holy thoughts
    intent,
    Upon the path a poor dead dog they
    spied:
One spurned him with his foot as on he
    went,
    And "What an ugly beast," another cried.

But in their Master's eyes compassion
   shone;
He stooped and touched the creature's
   shaggy head,
"At least, my dear disciples, you will own
His teeth are white as pearls," He
   gently said.

Then they passed on.   Dears, is it strange
   to you
That mothers with their babies round
   Him pressed?
That Peter learned to be so good and
   true,
And John leaned close upon His loving
   breast?

PLOUGHED UNDER.

IT grieves me much, the homes
    that I have spoiled,
    Of nest and burrow;
As in my barley-field to-day I toiled,
    Ploughing the furrow.

Armies of ants that grain by grain had
    laid
    Their snug embankment,
Were overwhelmed by my unhappy
    raid —
    Fort and encampment.

The silver ropes a cunning gymnast spun
    Met such disaster
That a wise fly who watched the spider
    run,
    Buzzed out with laughter!

Beneath a roof, where dandelion stars
    The rafters gilded,
Secured by no distrustful bolts or bars,
    Some birds had builded.

I peeped within, despite a sentry bold
    Of doughty metal,
Whose stinging impudence I knew of
    old —
    His name was Nettle!

It was not his rude protest made me spare
    My sparrow tenants;
I vanquished him, but left still fluttering
    there
    The flower pennants.

And oh! I grieve that I who hate to
    roam
    From my own burrow,
Have turned blind little moles out of their
    home
    Beneath my furrow!

WAITING.

HEN the crickets chirp in the
evening
And the stars flash out in the
sky,
Lonely I sit in my doorway
And watch the children go by;
I look at their fresh young faces,
And hark to each merry word,
For to me a child's own language
Is the sweetest ever heard.

I sit in my lonely doorway
In the hour that I love the best,
And think, as I see them passing,
My child will come with the rest;
Think, as I hear the clicking
Of the little garden gate,
My darling's hand is upon it —
Oh, why has she come so late?

But the days have been slowly weaving
    Their warp of toil in my life;
The weeks have brought me their burden
    Of waiting and patience and strife;
The flowers that came with the sunshine
    Have finished their errand so sweet,
And Autumn is dropping her harvests
    Mellow and ripe at my feet.

And yet my little girl comes not,
    So I think she has missed her way,
And strayed from this cold, dark country
    To one of perpetual day.
Perhaps. But I long to enfold her,
    To tangle my hand in her hair,
To feast my starved mouth on her kisses,
    To hear her light foot on the stair.

Some day I am sure I shall find her,
    But the road is lonesome between,
My spirit grows sick and impatient
    For glimpses of pastures so green;

Waiting I sit in the doorway,
In the hour my heart loves best,
And think, when the children pass home-
ward,
My child will come with the rest.

IN VANITY FAIR.

GRANDMOTHER sits in the cor-
    ner there
    Watching the comers to Vanity
    Fair,
For Madame, her daughter, "receives"
    to-day,
And a throng of carriages bars the way;
While color and perfume, and rare waltz-
    note
In my lady's corridors blend and float.

Yes, grandmother calls it "Vanity Fair,"
As she views the scene from her cushioned
    chair;
With a curious shadow of grave surprise
Troubling the depths of her fine old eyes
At the shimmering robes, the laces fine,
And the splendid jewels that flash and
    shine.

As she watches her daughter *débonnaire*,
Greeting the guests to Vanity Fair,
Does she not look like a picture old,
With her stiff brocade, and her kerchief's
    fold?
Or a somewhat prim, old-fashioned flower
In the hot-house air of my lady's bower?

Standing under the candles' flare,
In the tinted light of Vanity Fair,
Is her granddaughter, with eyes so blue
That a pair of stars mistook their hue
For the larger heavens and softly hid   .
Behind the cloud of each snowy lid!

And grandmother sighs with a troubled air
"They will spoil you, dear, in Vanity
    Fair;
They will brush the dew from your youth,
    I know,
And I trust not fully the handsome beau
Who bent to your hand with so fine a bow
And gave you the crimson rose but now?"

And she mutters, "Poor little fly, take care
Of the webs they weave in Vanity Fair!"
And no philosopher in the land
Could make this grandmother understand
That Vanity Fair, with its tricks and ways,
Was much the same in her younger days.

Grandmother, brooding on days that were,
You are out of place in Vanity Fair!
As a sweet old psalm is out of chime
With a prancing tune, or a laughing
    rhyme;
You are out of place in this modern room
With its garish light, and its rich perfume.

Let us wheel you out of the aching glare
From the lights and sounds of Vanity
    Fair;
Up the stairs to the restful gloom
Of your own old-fashioned, quiet room,
Where the same clock ticks the hours
    away
That wakened you on your wedding-day.

Let us leave all schemes that vex and
    snare
To the belles and beaux of Vanity Fair.
You have had your day; now your night
    is near,
Let us come away to your chamber here,
Where peaceful slumber your eyes invite,
Turn the light low; sleep well; good-
    night!

IF.

I F, sitting with this little worn-out
    shoe
    And scarlet stocking lying on
    my knee,
I knew the careless feet had pattered
    through
    The pearl - set gates that lie 'twixt
    Heaven and me,
And I could see beyond the mists of blue
    God's tender hand, I could submissive
    be.

If, in the morning, when the song of birds
    Reminds me of a music far more sweet,
I listen for his pretty broken words
    And for the music of his dimpled feet,
I could be almost happy, though I heard
    No answer, and but saw his vacant seat.

I could be glad, if, when the day is done,
    And all its cares and heartaches laid
        away,
I could look westward to the hidden sun,
    And, with a heart full of sweet yearn-
        ings, say,
" To-night I'm nearer to my little one
    By just the travel of a single day."

If I could know those little feet were shod
    In sandals wrought of light in better
        lands,
And that the foot-prints of a tender God
    Ran side by side with his in golden
        sands,
I could bow cheerfully and kiss the rod,
    Knowing he was in wiser, safer hands.

If he had died, as little children do,
    I would not stain the wee sock on my
        knee
With bitter tears, nor kiss the empty shoe

And cry, " Bring back my little boy
    to me ! "
I could be patient, until patience grew
Into the gladness of Eternity.

But oh, to know the feet once pure and
    white,
  The haunts of vice have boldly ven-
    tured in !
The hands that should have battled for
    the right
  Have been wrung crimson in the clasp
    of sin !
And should he knock at Heaven's gate
    to-night,
  My boy, alas, could scarce an entrance
    win !

BUDGE, TOM, AND HONEST JOE.

ITHIN it wanted just an hour of
    four;
Without, the world in summer
    beauty lay,
And wistfully beyond the school-room
    door
Budge, Tom, and Joseph looked this
    hot June day.

They knew that in the fields the clover
    spread
A rosy carpet, velvety and sweet;
They knew the path that to the old bridge
    led,
Where children loved to sit and swing
    their feet.

They knew that cherries hung upon the
    trees,
That   trusting   fishes   swarmed   the
    singing brook;
The robins seemed to call them from the
    leaves,
"Come out! Come out! and leave
    that hateful book!"

Budge dropped his drowsy head upon his
    breast,
Tom watched a fly upon the window-
    pane,
While Joseph, less lethargic than the rest,
Made horrid faces at his sister Jane.

The teacher saw the action with a smile,
    Their flushed young faces made her
    pitiful;
"Which will you do, go out and play
    awhile,
    Or stay with me," she said, "till close
    of school?"

Budge raised his sleepy head with glad
    surprise,
  (Just then a robin past the doorway
    flew!)
He choked, grew rosy red, then dropped
    his eyes;
  "I guess — I'd rather — stay in here —
    with you."

"And you, my Tommy?"   Should not
    Tommy dare
  To follow whither Spartan Budge had
    led?
(The robin called, the sky was oh, so
    fair!)
  "I'll stay with — Budge, I guess," he
    gasping said.

But Joseph, with a look half bold, half
    shy,
  His brown toes twisting in an awkward
    way,

Said, with a slight contempt in tone and
  eye,
"There ain't no use to talk, *I 'd* rather
  play."

The teacher smiled; " I fear, my little Joe,
  You only have been honest of the three.
I take each at his word; so you may go,
  While Budge and Tommy will remain
  with me."

Poor little boys! for such a sacrifice
  This was a fee they could not understand;
But when they said good night she kissed
  them thrice,
  And patted each round head with
  gentle hand.

And were they wholly wrong, and Joe all
  right?
  I leave the answer for your tongues to
  fill.

Talk it all over by the fire to-night,
And gather from the story what you
will.

But often do the world's sweet flatteries
Remind me of a day long years ago,
Around which cluster funny memories
Of three small boys, Budge, Tom, and
honest Joe.

IN MEMORY OF MR. CROWLEY OF CENTRAL PARK.

NO citizen of inferior name
    Has yielded up life's languid
    spark,
But a chimpanzee of goodly fame,—
    Mr. Crowley of Central Park,
Who from interior Africa came.

Many a slave of the pen we see,
    Who scribbles away from dawn till dark,
Nor earns the fame of this chimpanzee,
    Who could neither write nor make his
    mark,
Paradoxical though it be.

Many a player his lines may croon,
    Nor happily win, when his form lies
    stark,

An editorial in the *Tribune*
  Like Mr. Crowley of Central Park,
Late trapeze player!   Poor dead buffoon!

And many a poacher upon life's joys,
  Bagging his spoils with a snarl and bark,
To meaner purpose his life employs
  Than Mr. Crowley of Central Park; —
Jester at court of the girls and boys.

For a chimpanzee that can cheat dull care,
  And break a tooth of that hungry shark;
Who lightens the pack that the poor must
      bear
  Like Mr. Crowley of Central Park,
Is a better thing than the poacher there.

No more, poor clown, will your pranks
      beguile
  Life's weary labor and ceaseless cark;
You will be set up in a life-like style,
  And hold *levees* in a crystal ark,
With a very fixed and *blasé* smile.

Then, *au revoir*, with a kind regret !
Death interfered in your jolly lark,
And many a child's dear eyes· are wet
For Mr. Crowley of Central Park, —
The dearest monkey they ever met !

LININGS.

NAY, nay, dear child, I cannot let
you slight
Those inner stitches on your
gown's fair hem
Because, you say, they will be out of sight,
And no stern critic will discover them.

You do but build a most inviting hedge,
Behind which falsehood and deceit may
lurk,
When you embroider fair the outer edge,
And to the inner give no honest work.

The silken chain of habit which you wear
So lightly now upon your careless youth
Will strengthen strand by strand; then
have a care!
Else it may throttle the sweet soul of
truth.

I hold that every stitch untruly set
  Weaves a soiled thread along your web
    of fate;
And each deceitful seam may prove a
  net
  To hurt and hinder, trust me, soon or
    late.

Ah, dearest child, on everything you do
  Let the white seal of honor stamp its
    grace.
Keep all your soul as clean with heaven's
  dew
  As the pink flower of your tender
    face.

God makes no clumsy linings. Mark this
    bloom!
  A " fairy's glove; " and though it grieves
    my heart
To send the smallest blossom to its
  tomb,
  We 'll tear this dainty little glove apart.

In this and every flower that we behold,
  From crimson rose to pansy's purple
    vest,
God sews the velvet on the inner fold,
  And makes His linings fairer than the
    rest.

Is it not perfect, from the slender stem
  To the brown dapples on the curling
    rim?
God folds not carelessly the foxglove's
    hem;
  Then try, my little child, to be like
    Him.

A PRAYER.

OH, long strong breaths of salt sea
  air,
  Oh, north winds rough and
  south winds fair,
Toss all your rosy gifts about,
And blow afar our weary doubt!

Milk-white foam roses, break for me
From the green gardens of the sea,
And bring thy fragrance, briny sweet,
To wrap our love from brow to feet!

Bring rosy color to her mouth;
And from the warm and humid South
Waft spices to the fevered breath,
And antidote the spell of death!

And from thy green o'erflowing cup
My hand shall dip a potion up,
And in thy wine, to thee I 'll quaff
With relish sweet and joyous laugh.

Then bring to her the jewel health.
For naught of all thy treasured wealth
Is half so precious as this pearl —
This drooping lily of a girl!

A LITTLE CYNIC.

DANDELION and clover-top,
   Growing close together,
   Bobbed their bright young heads
    and talked
In the sweet spring weather.

Just across the little path
   In a grassy hollow,
Buttercup was coquetting
   With a noisy swallow.

" Do you know," said Dandelion,
   Growing stiff and sullen,
" That this minx, who used to rank
   With milk-weed and mullein,

" Goes to parties, *matinées*,
   And all such queer places,
And is quite the rage they say,
   With her airs and graces? "

" Well," laughed Clover, merrily,
 " This will we agree on,
That she wears her honors well
 For such a plebeian !

" I should quite disgrace myself—
 Spill my dew at dinner,
When it comes to etiquette
 I 'm a dreadful sinner."

" There is Madam Hollyhock,"
 Still pursued the other,
" Used to be on friendly terms
 With my great grandmother.

" Then she wore a narrow skirt
 With a simple tunic ;
Now she looks like some grand dame
 Just arrived from Munich !

" Then she leant upon the wall
 Or the lattice, may be,
Now she rings the front door bell
 Just like any lady ! "

"Why, you must be jealous, dear!"
　　Clover said serenely;
"For her colors are superb,
　　And her manners queenly.

"Her quaint bodice of pale green
　　Fits her to perfection,
And a ruffle more or less
　　Is no great objection."

Just then Violet passed by
　　In her soft, blue bonnet;
Dandelion's face grew dark
　　With the frown upon it.

"See!" she cried, "the whole, glad world
　　Greets her as she passes,
While our lives are hidden here
　　In the weeds and grasses!

"How I hate her artless ways!
　　Hate her queer poke bonnet!
Hate her modest drooping face,
　　With the soft smile on it!

"' Modest Violet,' indeed,
  When her very glory
Is the meek humility
  Granted her in story!

"Tell me, does God love her best?
  Count her blue gown fairer?
Are her graces sweet to Him?
  Is her perfume rarer?"

"Hush!" said Clover, sweetly grave,
  "God is God forever;
Doubt whatever else you will,
  But His goodness never!

"Violet gives lavishly
  Of her wealth of sweetness;
And the world requites the debt
  From its own completeness.

"Do not wrong the God above
  And our brown earth-mother.
Why not like your own life best,
  Sighing for no other?

" I would never change my lot
  With my wild bee lover
For a world of violets;
  No, not I ! " trilled Clover.

" Humph ! " that little cynic said
  With her bright eyes closing;
And the rest I never heard,
  For she fell a-dozing.

7

CHRISTMAS EVE.

OD bless the little stockings
    All over the land to-night,
    Hung in the choicest corners
In a glow of crimson light!
The tiny scarlet stocking,
    With a hole in heel and toe,
Worn by wonderful journeys
    The darlings have had to go.

And Heaven pity the children,
    Wherever their home may be,
Who wake at the first gray dawning
    An empty stocking to see,
Left in the faith of childhood
    Hanging against the wall,
Just where the dazzling glory
    Of Santa's light will fall!

Alas, for the lonely mother
  Whose home is empty and still,
Who has no scarlet stockings
  With childish toys to fill!
But sits in the deepening twilight,
  With her face against the pane,
And grieves for the little baby
  Whose grave lies out in the rain!

O empty shoes and stockings,
  Forever laid aside!
The tangled, broken shoe-strings
  That will never more be tied!
O little graves, at the mercy
  Of the cold December rain!
The feet in their snow-white sandals,
  That never can trip again!

But happier they who slumber
  With marble at foot and head,
Than the child who has no shelter,
  No raiment, nor food, nor bed.

Yes! Heaven help the living!
Children of want and pain,
Knowing no fold nor pasture —
Outside to-night in the rain!

JAMIE'S PRAYER.

DAY'S weary burdens are laid by;
    The world's great throbbing
      heart is still;
The stars flash out, the moon's fair face
    Rests on the peak of yonder hill.

I hear the katydids contend
    The rustling maple leaves among;
And leaning toward the apple boughs,
    I hear the robin brood her young.

It is the hour when children's prayers
    Like perfume from the lilies rise,
When all the angels cry, " Oh, list ! "
    And God makes silence in the skies.

Two small brown hands, unsoiled by sin,
    Are folded softly on my knee,
And over them my child's dear head
    Is bowed in sweet humility.

Hark to the little honest prayer !
  "Dear God, I am too tired to pray,
And 't ain't as if you did n't know
   Just all I 've said and done to-day.

"I know it takes a sight of love
  To make a boy's sins white, but then
You don't go back on what you say,
  And I am not afraid — Amen."

SHOCKING!

THE smallest wheel in the rector's
  clock,
 The busiest worker in that queer
  mill,
Grew tired of hearing the same tick-tock,
 So a Sunday morning it stood stock-
  still!
And what befell?   Why, the rector good
 Arrived at his church full a half hour
  late,
With a flying gown — as no parson
  should —
 While all the parish amazed did wait.

With childish wonder our little Sue,
 Who never had been in a church before
Saw, from her high-backed, oaken pew,
 The rector enter the chancel door.

The wonder grew in the child's brown
    eyes,
What she was thinking we could not tell,
But a look of shame and of shocked sur-
    prise
Over her face like a shadow fell.

"What did you see at the church, my
    sweet?"
Said grandmother, kissing the lifted chin,
When at dinner the two did meet.
    "Oh, grandma! the preacher came
    flying in,
So late that he did n't get on his clothes,
    And had just a great, long nightgown on;
He had to hurry so, I suppose!"
    Said the innocent child, while her round
    eyes shone.

"I guess he was drefful ashamed of hisself;
    Would n't *you* be, grandma, in his place?
For he knelt right down on a little shelf,
    And held his two hands over his face!

And, grandma, it was a minute before
  He would lift his head and read from
    his book.
He'll not wear his nightgown, I guess
  any more.
    Oh, dear!" and she sighed, "how queer
    it did look!"

THE SCARECROW.*

THOREAU surveyed the effigy
with scorn.
"Well! well!" laughed he, "some
urchin must have planned
This man of straw.   No crow in all the
land
Was ever frightened from a feast of corn
By such a sentinel.   No blackbird born
Would hesitate to perch upon its hand.
Crows are too knowing not to under-
stand
That this poor, stuffed-out thing, battered
and worn,
With dangling arms and shapeless,
jointless pegs,
Was never made by God."   Thoreau
paused here

* A true anecdote of Thoreau.

In his wise dissertation upon crows;
For lo! the scarecrow moved its "joint-
less" legs
And walked away to a gray farmhouse
near.
That *was* a funny blunder of Thoreau's!

IF WE KNEW.

F we knew the baby fingers
    Pressed against the window-
       pane
Would be cold and stiff to-morrow —
    Never trouble us again;.
Would the bright eyes of our darling
    Catch the frown upon our brow?
Would the prints of rosy fingers
    Vex us then as they do now?

Ah, these little ice-cold fingers,
    How they point our memories back
To the hasty words and actions
    Strewn along our backward track!
How these little hands remind us,
    As in snowy grace they lie,
Not to scatter thorns — but roses —
    For our reaping by and by!

Strange we never prize the music
　Till the sweet-voiced bird has flown;
Strange that we should slight the violets
　Till the lovely flowers are gone;
Strange that summer skies and sunshine
　Never seem one-half so fair
As when winter's snowy pinions
　Shake their white down in the air!

Lips from which the seal of silence
　None but God can roll away,
Never blossomed in such beauty
　As adorns the mouth to-day;
And sweet words that freight our memory
　With their beautiful perfume,
Come to us in sweeter accents
　Through the portals of the tomb.

Let us gather up the sunbeams
　Lying all around our path;
Let us keep the wheat and roses,
　Casting out the thorns and chaff;

Let us find our sweetest comfort
In the blessings of to-day;
With a patient hand removing
All the briars from our way.

A LITTLE ROBBER.

LITTLE robber whom I know
  Came to my house nine years
      ago,
And, with the most provoking ease,
Found out my casket and my keys,
And of the treasures I possessed
Purloined the dearest and the best.
The way this robber came to me
Is wrapped in sweetest mystery;
But the bewitching little thief,
Without remorse or touch of grief,
First stole, in many a pretty way,
Three times eight jewels every day;
Then, with his soft and rosy hands,
He pulled down all my strong commands,
The cherished plan, the ripened thought,
By years of rich experience bought.
My favorite opinions, too,
He into wildest chaos threw.

Some prim old maxims, quaintly wrought
With silver thread and pious thought,
By long consent had grown to be
Proud souvenirs of ancestry ;
These, by mere love of mischief led,
He picked to pieces thread by thread,
Until I feared my grandma's ghost
Would chain me to a whipping-post!
When I reproached, his wondrous eyes
Took on such look of grieved surprise,
I could but say, " Take what you will,
Your plunderings continue still;
Purloin my time, my heart, my pelf,
Take everything except — yourself!
For what would all earth's treasures be
Without your blessed company?"

And so, throughout the years and days,
Content this young marauder stays,
To be my comfort and my joy,
His name?   Why, he's my little boy!

"SUFFER LITTLE CHILDREN TO COME UNTO ME."

T was long years ago that He uttered
   This message, so tender and sweet,
As women were crowding about Him
   And laying their babes at His feet;
He looked, with a gentle compassion,
   On the mothers in old Galilee,
While He comforted them with this saying,
   "Let the little ones come unto me."

From over the hills of Judea,
   Down through the long line of the years,
That Voice of ineffable sweetness
   Still comforts the mother's sad tears.
O Heart that has bled for our sorrows!
   O Voice that can quiet the sea!
Come often to *me* with Thy whisper:
   "Let the little ones come unto me!"

8

O mothers, whose children are lying
   Out under the snow and the rain,
Let the beautiful words of the Master,
   Give ease to your sorrow and pain!
He holds their bright heads on His bosom,
   He gathers them close to His knee ;
And tenderly still He is saying,
   " Let the little ones come unto me ! "

"A LITTLE CHILD SHALL LEAD THEM."

"THE land is wondrous fair," the
    angel said.
  "Its sapphire skies are wrought
    with tints of gold;
Its jewelled gates admit nor heat nor
    cold;
And all along the way that you shall
    tread
A perfume marvellously sweet is shed
From lilies that eternally unfold."

The lovely woman raised her timid face,
    And to the messenger of death she
        spoke:
  "I know that human sight can not
    invoke

A vision of such fair, surpassing grace,
As those fair mansions in the heavenly
place,
But life and I have never friendship
broke.

" Therefore I fain would stay," she pleaded
low.
The angel's ˗ face wore nothing of
command ;
He smiling said, " Behold, unarmed I
stand !
I left behind my arrows and my bow.
I shall not force you, lovely one, to go ;
I only wait till you shall clasp my
hand.

" But even now your eyes are wet with
tears :
Come where a holy hand will wipe them
dry !
Oh, be my bride, my own beloved ! and I

Will kiss away your doubtings and your
    fears,
And lead you gently through the eternal
    · years,
    And prove a love that will not change
      or die ! "

The woman shrank from his caressing hand.
    " But life hath loyal love as well," she
      cried ;
    " A trusting heart would break of me
      denied ;
A faithful foot would track me to your
    land.
And at the gates of pearl would waiting
    stand.
    This life is fair and sweet to me," she
      sighed.

" The swaying reed hath not a frailer grace
    Than human love. It will not mourn
      you long;
    In Heaven your voice is needed in the
      song.

Through countless ages God has kept your
   place.
Then, in my bosom hide your weeping
   face,
   And let me bear you to the waiting
   throng."

" Nay, nay, sweet angel! Spare me this
   alarm;
   For I am timid of the lonesome way.
   A voice I love is begging me to stay!
A precious hand is clinging to my arm, —
A hand that never brought me pain or
   harm!
   Oh, leave me now, and come another
   day!"

The angel drew her close and whispered
   sweet,
   " Dear Heart! the streets are fair with
   children there,
   God's sunlight hides its kisses in their
   hair,

And everywhere in Heaven a child you
    meet."
The woman clasped his hand, and toward
    the street
So bright with children, smiling went
    the pair.

OUR BOBBY WAS PINCHING THE KITTEN.

UR Bobby was pinching the kitten,
    And kicking his primer about,
    And pulling a beetle to pieces,
His face all awry in a pout;
His mother, who, patient and loving,
    Could coax her dear Bobby no more,
Now reached for the whip on the mantel —
And looked at her boy on the floor.

But grandma, with soft, muslin kerchief
    Pinned over her warm, loving breast,
Where ten little heads had been pillowed
    And rocked into childhood's sweet rest,
Looked up from the little wool stocking
    Just finished and laid on her knee,
And said, " Dear, you 'll ruin his temper,
    You had far better let the child be.

"Don't whip him — his father before him
　　Was punished and shut in the dark,
And stood on one foot in the corner,
　　And disciplined up to the mark;
We gave him no credit for honor,
　　But watched him as spiders watch flies.
I wonder that it did n't teach him
　　To practise deceit and tell lies.

" We called it affection and duty —
　　God knows we were fond of the boy —
But I guess his remembrance of child-
　　　　hood
　　Is not quite a well-spring of joy.
So put up that willow whip, daughter,
　　And try little Bobby once more.
You see he 's forgotten his passion,
　　And lies half asleep on the floor."

Then grandmother lifted her darling,
　　And patted his head on her breast,
And sang in a tremulous treble,
　　Till all Bobby's woes were at rest.

And so the wee whip, bright and yellow,
Was laid on the mantel again —
And that is the way that the grandmas
Spoil nine little boys out of ten.

HE KNOWS BEST.

IF I could utter some new magic
    word
  To lull the pain in one poor
    troubled soul ;
Or when Bethesda's shining pool is stirred
  Could lift some cripple in and make
    him whole ;

If I could set some bruised and tired feet
  Where they could henceforth tread a
    smoother way,
I would not ask a gift more fair and
    sweet,
  To bless me on this happy Christmas
    day.

Ah, foolish heart, be still ! Nor any
    more
Distrust the tenderness that is divine !

He knows wherever feet are bruised and
   sore,
   And gives them pity, gentler far than
   thine.

Our keenest sorrow may be sent to bring
   The dearest guest our life has ever
   known, —
Sweet patience, who in gathering the sting
   From other's lives forgets about her own.

And there are *old* sweet words of truth
   and love,
   As full of meaning as a mother's kiss,
Which fall like benedictions from above,
   And never weary in a world like this.

Bethesda's pool is nearer than we think,
   It springs wherever there are tired feet;
The gift you crave lies trembling on its
   brink,
   You still may make your Christmas day
   complete !

And though it may be hard to understand
The way through which He leads your
life and mine,
May we not safely trust the gracious hand
That brings to us so good a Christmas
time?

COMFORT.

I F I could lay my hand upon the
heart
That moulders underneath the
·church-yard snows,
And bid the sleeping pulses wake and start,
And to the faded lips restore the rose;

If I could lead the precious child you love
With shrinking footsteps to his earthly
place;
If I could bring him from the fold above,
The tangled paths of life again to trace;

Say! would you bid him lay his glory by
That you might hold him to your
troubled breast?
And would your yearning mother-heart
deny
The good to him that you might thus
be blest?

I know your answer! Tenderly enough
  Has God's sweet mercy through His
    smiting shone.
Young feet are tender, and the way is
    rough ;
  Be glad that you can tread the thorns
    alone !

It is not long. The way is short between,
  And we are near the gates of pearl and
    gold ; .
And yonder rise the hills of living green,
  Where children never die, nor yet grow
    old !

And when the storms shall beat, and rains
    shall fall,
  And when you faint beneath the sun's
    fierce ray,
O friend be glad ! and sing above it all,
  " My child is safe from all these ills
    to-day ! "

A SUBPŒNA.

BOISTEROUS Wind! Prince
Weather's clown!
You have raised such a breeze
in Blossom-town,
That the undersigned bid you appear
And answer the charges mentioned here.

Robin is there quite red in the breast
With rage, at the loss of a brand-new nest.

Bumble-bee draggled from sting to chin
Crawls from the pool you tumbled him in.

Violet looks *so* wicked and sly
With her tattered bonnet blown all awry!

Hyacinth, blue, and with head cast down,
Has a breadth torn out of her bell-shaped
gown.

Butterfly holds up a crippled wing; —
(How *could* you spoil such a dainty thing?)

Some sweet young buds that were coming
 out
Fetchingly gowned for their opening rout,

You whirled away to a dance of your own
With never a sign of a chaperone!

And worst of all, in your headlong race
You drew your switches across the face

Of that pet of the forest, Anemone,
Bravest and frailest of flowers that be.

Then haste, rude Jester! Prince Weather's
 clown!
By the air-line route to Blossom-town.
For, I give you warning, there's much
 ado
In the circles there, on account of you.

DEPARTING DAY.

WHILE children lean their cheeks in
    drowsy prayer
  Against their mother's knees, and
    all the air
Is sweet with vesper bell;
See, the spent Day faints on the sunset
    strand,
Her smouldering torch down-drooping
    from her hand
In token of farewell!

With vague regret I watch each ebbing
    grace:
Come Twilight, gentle nun! before her
    face
Shall cold and ashen be;

Fold thy gray veil above her as she lies,
And sprinkle her with dews from thy soft
eyes;
She hath been kind to me.

THE END.

www.ingramcontent.com/pod-product-compliance
Lightning Source LLC
Chambersburg PA
CBHW020507270326
41926CB00008B/772